RU

RUNHUNDRED

HEART VERSUS HEAT AT WESTERN STATES 100

CHRIS ZEHETLEITNER

THE PATH
· PUBLISHING ·

The Path Publishing
www.thepathpublishing.com

Cover design and illustrations by Alessandro Locatelli / Papermoustache
Editing by Christine Bucher
Proofreading by Stefan Vonbun

ISBN: 978-3-9825936-0-9 (Paperback edition)
ISBN: 978-3-9825936-1-6 (Ebook edition)

For Lisa. The love of my life.

CONTENTS

WESTERN STATES ENDURANCE RUN

DISTANCE	**100.2 MI**
ASCENT	**18.090 FT**
DESCENT	**22.970 FT**

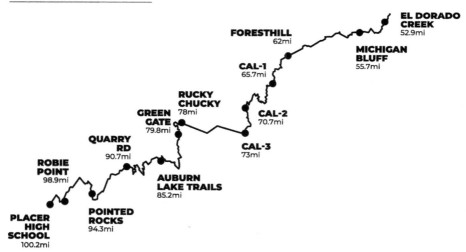

EL DORADO CREEK
52.9mi

FORESTHILL
62mi

MICHIGAN BLUFF
55.7mi

CAL-1
65.7mi

RUCKY CHUCKY
78mi

GREEN GATE
79.8mi

CAL-2
70.7mi

QUARRY RD
90.7mi

CAL-3
73mi

ROBIE POINT
98.9mi

AUBURN LAKE TRAILS
85.2mi

PLACER HIGH SCHOOL
100.2mi

POINTED ROCKS
94.3mi

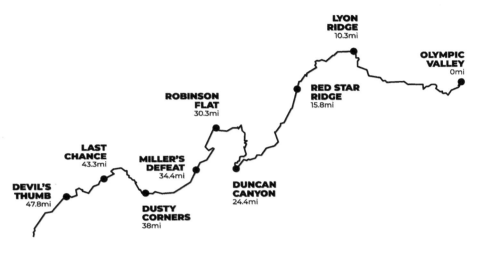

OLYMPIC VALLEY 0mi

LYON RIDGE 10.3mi

RED STAR RIDGE 15.8mi

ROBINSON FLAT 30.3mi

LAST CHANCE 43.3mi

MILLER'S DEFEAT 34.4mi

DEVIL'S THUMB 47.8mi

DUSTY CORNERS 38mi

DUNCAN CANYON 24.4mi

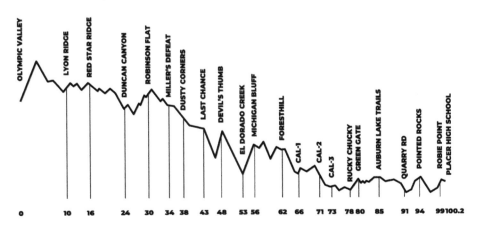

OLYMPIC VALLEY · LYON RIDGE · RED STAR RIDGE · DUNCAN CANYON · ROBINSON FLAT · MILLER'S DEFEAT · DUSTY CORNERS · LAST CHANCE · DEVIL'S THUMB · EL DORADO CREEK · MICHIGAN BLUFF · FORESTHILL · CAL-1 · CAL-2 · CAL-3 · RUCKY CHUCKY · GREEN GATE · AUBURN LAKE TRAILS · QUARRY RD · POINTED ROCKS · ROBIE POINT · PLACER HIGH SCHOOL

0   10 16   24   30 34 38   43 48   53 56   62   66   71 73 78 80   85   91 94 99 100.2

"Ich kenn die Panik ich kenn den Mut./ War kurz im Himmel ewig in der Hölle./ War mal die Flamme mal kalte Glut./ Ich kenn die Ebbe./ Ich kenn die Flut."

SLIME, *EBBE & FLUT*

"I know the panic, I know the courage./ I was in heaven and forever in hell./ I was the flame and the cold embers./ I know the ebb./ I know the flow."

FOREWORD

BY HENNING LENERTZ

I didn't cry when my dog died, or when I graduated from high school, or when my five-year-long relationship failed. Or when I married my wife. All these events, happy and sad, usually make people cry. In such situations, I ask myself if I am different from everyone else. Are my responses inappropriate? Do I lack empathy or emotions? Is something wrong with me?

That might be true in some ways. But there is a specific situation that does make me cry. The first time it happened was in 2015 when I finished the Transalpine Run, an eight-day stage-race across the Alps. At the finish, tears suddenly appeared. Embarrassed by the sudden emotion, I tried to hide them, not because I am a man and "men do not cry." (That's bullshit!) I was embarrassed because I had no clue *why* I was crying. There was no obvious reason. After a few minutes, my tears dried, and I could rejoice with my team partner, Jenson. The second time was in 2018, at the Stubai Ultratrail. Kneeling in the snow at the finish, 3,100 meters above sea level, I just wept — and for such a long time that the race medics asked me twice if everything was alright. Everything was alright, indeed. The next year, at the Amsterdam Marathon, it happened even before the finish. I sobbed so much I was nearly blind as I ran the last 300 meters in the Olympic Stadium.

Why did these races move me to tears? Other races have been much more successful, harder, or longer, yet I didn't cry. Sure, I was either happy to have reached my goal or unhappy when I missed it. After my first 100-km race, I was even a bit disappointed that I *didn't* cry. Even I know that being disappointed is a rather inappropriate feeling when you've accomplished such a big running goal, something you have trained for and managed to achieve with no problems and much faster than expected.

It took me a long time to find out why some races move me to tears, while most others don't. That is when I have to drag myself out of deep physical lows, when I face deep inner struggles and really push my boundaries. It's when I have to accomplish something that I didn't think was possible before. But when a race runs smoothly, there are no tears.

There was one other situation in which I got very emotional. It was at the Western States Endurance Run 2019. I was a crew member for my friend Josef. I paced him for 52 km from Foresthill to Pointed Rocks. And when he crossed the finish line after 23 hours and 9 minutes, I had to cry. Witnessing how he suffered through his physical low points, fought the battles within himself, and kept pushing his boundaries touched me as deeply as if I had run those 100 miles myself. Since that day, Western States is much more than just an iconic race to me. It's on the very top of my running and life-goals bucket list. To be honest, it's the only thing left on that list.

Therefore, I didn't have to think twice when Chris asked me if I wanted to be a part of his crew for his 2022 Western States race. There was only one plausible answer: it's Western States.

I would rather not spoil anything that Chris, his crew, and I experienced during our trip to California. Just one thing I want to say: it meant a lot to me to be part of all this.

It's easy to say that something means a lot to you. It is much harder to explain *why* it has so much meaning. The same goes for people who we love, music we listen to and, crucial for us runners, the races we want to run and the personal goals we hope to reach. Meaningfulness is individual. Meaningfulness is irrational. Meaningfulness is subjective. Meaningfulness is emotional. We can charge a thing with meaning, yet that same thing leaves everyone else completely unaffected. And that is why you might read this book and simply like it. However, you might well shed some tears while reading this. Just like I did.

— *Henning Lenertz, Runner's World editor*

PRELUDE

THE COOLER DIALOGUE

I was sitting on a cooler at an aid station, partway through a race I had given up on. My head buried in my hands as my wife, Lisa, kneeled in front of me, her hands on my knees. I told her, "I'm done. This is over. I wish I had more grit, like all those other runners. But I have nothing left. I'm so empty."

Tears ran over my face as I spoke these words, followed by an occasional burst of shivering and cramping, a condition I'd been struggling with for the last 10 hours. The unrelenting heat had undermined a good number of my bodily functions and my ability to eat or drink carbohydrates.

Lisa tried to persuade me to continue. "Don't you think it would be possible to get up and hike with me to Cal-1? It's only 3 miles and the course runs downhill. Should be a nice trip!"

"I think I could do that, but then what?," I replied. "I'll be stuck at Cal-1 with no one to pick me up there. I'd have to hike it all back up to Foresthill after I drop out at Cal-1. That'd be so humiliating…"

"Want some more soup? I'll be back soon, I'm just picking up my head lamp." Lisa wasn't going to give up on me.

"You don't get my point! The race is over. I'm far behind the 30-hour pace I need to finish this. I would have to run really fast for the rest of the race. I don't have another 38 miles in me. It's just not there." Again, I burst out in tears of anger and frustration.

Lisa embraced me, and I felt the warmth of her body. "You don't have to run 38 miles. Just 3. To the next aid station."

"But what for? What's the idea? Dropping out down there in the canyon is much more complicated than doing it up here at Foresthill!"

"Maybe you don't want to drop out when you're at Cal-1…"

My voice got adamant, and I deployed my all-business arguing tone: "Correct me if my calculations are wrong. I need to run an average pace of 11:10 to finish under 30 hours. We're now averaging an 11:35 pace. It's impossible to make up that gap. Even if I run fast, I need at least 10 to 15 minutes at every aid station to recover and get my shit together. It won't work. It's over. Period."

But Lisa would not engage with my smart-ass arguments. "Let's just try anyway. We could hike down to Cal-1 just for fun. You and me together. This time, I'll even bring my own head lamp!"

My voice, and my heart, softened slightly. "That would be really nice, but I still don't think you get my point. Even if I give it all, I won't make it to the finish in under 30 hours. I screwed that up hours ago in the heat. I cannot bring back the lost time anymore. My race is over. It's been over since Devil's Thumb."

Again, Lisa didn't engage. In fact, she acted as if I'd agreed with her plan, saying, "Here's your coffee, drink a sip. I'll be back with my head lamp in a second."

"Ok." What else could I say?

Her words were totally disarming. In a way, I felt manipulated, deprived of the right to make my own decision. But at the same time, her compassion and attentiveness to my bad condition were real. Before I knew what was happening, Lisa and I were hiking out of the Foresthill aid station of the 2022 Western States Endurance Run, and I was back in the race that I had completely relinquished hours before.

Just moments later, I would find out I was wrong. About everything. My broken body and my clouded mind had tricked me into self-abandonment, yet my heart was still hungry to finish this race. It would soon carry me all the way through the night and to the Placer High School track in Auburn, California. Nothing short of a miracle — at least from the point of view of someone sitting on a cooler at Foresthill arguing about lost time, cutoffs, and average paces.

100

INTRODUCTION

> "One thing I noticed was that writing honestly about running and writing honestly about myself are nearly the same thing."
>
> — HARUKI MURAKAMI, *WHAT I TALK ABOUT WHEN I TALK ABOUT RUNNING*

OF MY RUNNING BUCKET LIST

My running bucket list has never been long. On it, I have a marathon in under 3 hours, a self-supported crossing of the Alps, 1,000 meters in under 3 minutes, returning to the Boston Marathon and finishing strong, and sometime in the distant future, running the Western States Endurance Run as my first 100-mile race.

I recently checked off the last thing on the list and wrote this book about the entire journey.

It's not unusual for runners to have Western States, short for Western States Endurance Run or Western States 100, on their bucket list. Even if you are not yet familiar with the sport of ultrarunning, you will, eventually, hear about this iconic race in the Sierra Nevada Mountains, which has a long history and is fairly rich in tradition. Once you dig deeper into the many extraordinary stories Western States has written over the decades, you'll most likely be hooked too. It happened to me while I was reading *Eat & Run,* by ultrarunning legend Scott Jurek. His fascinating career gained the greatest momentum when he raced and won Western States seven consecutive times between 1999 and 2005. He even held the male course record time of 15:36:27 for 6 years, from 2004 until 2010. But it was not his impressive results that fascinated me. It was Scott's meticulous description of the race and all its wonderful challenges, big and small. I also asked myself: why would a runner, who is in his absolute prime, return to the same race over and over again? The answer is obvious. Because it's Western States.

I read *Eat & Run* in 2014. At that time, I was a far cry from being an ultrarunner myself. I had just started running a couple of months before and was training for my first half-marathon. And yet, Scott Jurek's stories fascinated me. His words describing long days of running in the mountains of Colorado and California evoked an intriguing image of boundless freedom and adventurous independence in me.

My first contact with ultrarunning in the real world was through my newly emerged circle of running friends, the Willpower Athletes. In 2015, I built upon my many years of experience as a music business professional and founded my own running clothing company, called Willpower. A group of like-minded runners, who shared the same values, soon gathered under the banner of my emerging brand. This circle of friends soon became my most important connection to the world of running and tremendously influenced my practice of this sport.

Among the Willpower Athletes, it was quite common to run long distances. Most of these athletes were experienced ultra-runners, and a good number had already mastered 100-kilometer or even 100-mile (ca. 161 km) mountain races. Therefore, running ultramarathons was a normal topic of conversation. However, it took me another two years until I dared to tackle an ultra myself. In 2017, I ran the 65-kilometer distance at the Zugspitz Ultratrail in Garmisch-Partenkirchen, a ski resort town at the foot of Germany's highest mountain, the Zugspitze. It was unlike anything I had ever done before, and it became clear to me that running ultras wouldn't let me go. The large spectrum of emotions I went through, the profound sense of self-discovery, and the complete isolation from all everyday thoughts and concerns held a mesmerizing allure and touched my soul.

But even years later, following my first experiences with running beyond the 42.195-kilometer mark, I was not planning to do a 100-mile race any time soon. I was satisfied just switching back and forth between road races and trail running, with distances varying from 50 to 70 kilometers. That was my running horizon. There was still so much to discover and achieve for me. After all, I had only been a runner since 2013, and I felt that I wasn't yet mature enough for any distances longer than that. Yet still, Western States was always in the back of my mind, and we kept on crossing paths.

OF THE LEVELHEAD AND THE PUNK

Not going all-in immediately regarding ultrarunning also has something to do with my personality. Or should I say "personalit*ies*?" My running life — and really, all of my life — is epitomized by two hearts beating in my chest. I often call these two impulses the Levelhead and the Punk.

A part of me, the Levelhead, loves to thoroughly think things through, play it safe, plan meticulously, take long breaths, relax, and enjoy a predictable process. He lives in a world of numbers and data. The Levelhead is not easily thrown off-track. He is well organized, loves to apply his existing knowledge and, as his name implies, keeps a cool head. The Levelhead is the personification of order.

The other part of me, the Punk, loves to enter the void, to feel overwhelmed, and to exist in any place where uncertainty and havoc reign and where he is not the one in control. The Punk is relentlessly curious and typically reacts off-the-cuff. He fails a lot, then tries again with an almost childlike naivety. The Punk embodies chaos. But also pure love and fervor.

In my running world, the Levelhead stands for road racing, while the Punk embraces trail and ultrarunning. The Levelhead strives for all things to go as planned, while the Punk seeks the great unknown. The Levelhead runs with his mind. The Punk runs with his heart.

Another way to describe these two parts of my personality can be found in the words and concepts of psychologist C. G. Jung about the Ego and the Self.

The Ego is what we think of as "I," while the Self is a much more holistic concept. It's a greater entity which includes the Ego as well as the personal and collective conscious and the unconscious. It's a quasi-spiritual realm from which dreams, intuition, ideas, and infinite wisdom emerge. If this sounds too high-flying to you, you can consider the Self to be the soul, destiny, or the often invoked "something greater than ourselves."

In our everyday lives, the Ego sits in the driver's seat, and we wouldn't survive a single day if it didn't. And for good reason: the Ego is pragmatic and rational. It believes in physicality. Nothing exists but the material world, and everything is subject to its profane rules. There is nothing after death. Once we die, life ends.

The Self, on the contrary, is everything beyond the material world. It questions death, time, and space. On its hallowed ground, we are all one, connected by love. We humbly access the Self when we meditate, chant, or pray. Also, when we brainstorm, have a flash of inspiration in the shower or telepathically share the same thought at the same moment with another person. But most of all, the Self emerges when we perceive what is left when we believe nothing is left. This inexplicable mystic force is the Self.

There is a constant fight going on between the Ego and the Self. The Ego wants to keep things as they are. The Self intends to evolve, to learn, to grow.

The Levelhead inside of me gravitates toward the Ego. The Punk is drawn to the Self.

Don't worry — it's not schizophrenia. There is also no good or bad about these two parts of my personality. Both characters make up who I am. I constantly switch back and forth between the two. Sometimes the Levelhead is in the lead, and every so often the Punk takes over.

So maybe it was luck, or even destiny, that turned a dream in the distant future — a roll of the dice — into immediate reality. Against all odds, I won the Western States lottery and ended up on the 2022 entrants list of the race. This news really took me by surprise and overpowered me, to say the least. In fact, I had just finished the biggest running project of my life so far, my first 100-km ultramarathon, and was longing to enter my typical running safe zone, a well-structured and highly predictable road marathon training cycle. I wasn't ready for the next big thing.

When the Western States lottery results came in, there was stillness inside me. Neither the Levelhead nor the Punk dared to step forward. This running project was just too big to grasp for either of them, and for me.

It took me a while to process this piece of information. I had been granted the chance and the honor to run my first 100-mile race at Western States. But after a while, the Levelhead and the Punk slowly started raising their unique voices. Different perspectives and imaginations started taking turns. First it was the Punk, whose input mirrored the unknown sage who said, "Running a 100-miler can't be that hard. What's the harm?" As we leave our everyday lives to race an ultramarathon, we enter the underworld, the reign of chaos and unpredictability, home of the Punk. You don't know what is going to happen, but you better be prepared. But there's no fear. Ultrarunning is also a place to find, to discover, to surprise, in a positive and fulfilling way. It can enrich you. Even enlighten you, in some cases.

But the Levelhead emerged, using the words of the A-Team's Colonel John "Hannibal" Smith: "I love it when a plan comes together!" Maybe Col. Smith knew that preparing yourself for a 100-mile ultramarathon is one hell of a project. Especially if it is your first time running such a long distance. But fundamentally, it's not rocket science. The same rules of training theory apply to any running distance. Any sport, for that matter. There's also a great pool of knowledge out there about both running 100 miles in general and Western States in particular. All this aroused the curiosity and thirst for action of the Levelhead. Would it be indeed possible to tackle such a big race?

But the greatest truth came in the words of Yoda: "You must unlearn what you have learned."

I would soon find out that a well-planned training schedule, knowledge, and experience will bring the Levelhead to the start line. Self-confident and, without any doubt, well-prepared. However, I would reach a point in running Western States where this carefully built house of cards collapsed. I would have to let it, and myself, go. There would be a moment where I would need to leave behind what I knew and what I thought I knew. The Punk would take the helm.

There are countless ways to run a 100-mile ultramarathon, and even more reasons to do it. But the true reasons, I believe, are not to be found in your mind. They are enshrined in your heart. And they have been there since the day you decided to sign up.

Running an ultramarathon is pure bravery. It's doubt, it's death, it's rebirth, and a homecoming. A true hero's journey that might turn your life upside down. And this is the story I'd like to share with you.

OF THIS BOOK

This book is not about impressive numbers, flawless training logs, and stellar finishing times or placements. It's not going to tell the tale of a successful race that was well prepared for and even better executed. My story is rather about how I connected with what's deep inside of me, and that might inspire you to do the same, to find the good, the bad, the worse, the absolutely terrible and the disconcertingly ugly. But deep inside, you might also find an endless source of energy that does not follow any plausible logic. No previous race result, training performance, distance value, elevation profile, or race description will ever predict the outcome or experience of an ultramarathon. We're at the mercy of something bigger, and that's what makes this sport so unbelievably beautiful to me. And it's the reason this book exists.

Moreover, if you are looking for universal tips and tricks or a detailed manual for the Western States Endurance Run, you are also in the wrong place. I am not the right person to tell you how to train for or run this epic race. Or any race, for that matter. Even if I had tried to translate my Western States experiences into a runners' guide, it still would be mostly a "Do as I say, not as I do" kind of thing. I am by no means an experienced ultrarunner yet, and I'm the last one to tell you what to do and how to do it, as you'll see.

But if you're looking for the honest story of a deep dive into the heart and mind of an ambitious recreational athlete, who loves this sport to pieces, this is the book for you. A runner who, while preparing for and racing at Western States, discovered that an ultramarathon is not to be mastered only with well-thought-out plans, rational numbers, and calculations. It is to be run with the heart. A lesson that I certainly learned the hard way, but which changed my life forever.

This book is also a tribute to the most wonderful race I ever participated in. I will tell you how Western States left its mark on me. You might get an impression of why the Western States Endurance Run means so much to so many runners around the world and why it has grown from a single runner at its start in 1974 to the most renowned ultramarathon in the world. If you ever get the chance to participate in the race, no matter if it is as a runner, a volunteer, a pacer, a crew member, or even just as a spectator, you should not think twice. It's going to be an incredible experience. I promise you that.

And, if all goes well, my book can hopefully serve as an inspiration to you to follow your own running dreams. And a motivation to turn them into concrete goals to work toward. The same point where I was at in December 2021, when my Western States journey started.

So let's go to where it all began. In Chamonix, France.

100

PART ONE
CALL TO WESTERN STATES

CHAPTER 1
ONE HUNDRED...
KILOMETERS

> "To run 100 miles and more is to bring the body to the point of breaking, to bring the mind to the point of destruction, to arrive at that place where you can alter your consciousness."
>
> — SCOTT JUREK

Chamonix is a magical place, able to stir the heart of any curmudgeon. However, when I entered the Place du Triangle de l'Amitié, in the center of Chamonix, in the early morning hours of August 28, 2021, I was feeling nothing. Not necessarily a bad thing after running 100 kilometers (62 miles) around the Mont Blanc massif. At least I was not drowning in pain or fatigue or marked by hours of mental suffering. But there was also no overflowing joy, no great sense of relief, and no real feeling of accomplishment. I simply crossed the finish line, gave Lisa, who would soon be my fiancé, and my dad both a hug, sipped on a cup of cola and drove home. That was it.

I had run my first 100-kilometer ultramarathon, the CCC, at the UTMB, the biggest event in our sport. The CCC is the not-so-small little sister of UTMB, the Super Bowl of trail running, as it has been called many times. CCC isn't actually small: it features a whopping 20,000 feet (6100 m) of altitude gain and even more loss over its course. Held at high altitude, up to 8,500 feet (ca. 2600 m), runners usually face difficult and quickly changing weather conditions, rugged terrain and extremely long and steep climbs and descents, which makes the CCC a highly desirable race for almost every ultrarunner.

It had been on top of my own bucket list for a first 100-km race for a long time. However, I didn't plan to do it in 2021. I had just finished a pointless marathon training cycle with no proper conclusion. The marathon I'd wanted to race had been cancelled the second year in a row because of COVID-19. I was then, by surprise, lucky enough to enter a second signup for the highly sought after CCC race. I hadn't been selected in the initial race draw, but because numerous athletes had to cancel their trip due to the worldwide pandemic, the event organizers offered a second chance to enter. Within a 24-hour time window, everyone with enough points from official qualifying races could apply again for a chance to be selected to run their race of choice at UTMB. I won't go into more detail here — the UTMB registration and lottery is the most complicated in the world. Not even pro athletes, who make a living from running such races, fully understand how it works. But somehow I got one of these much-coveted spots to start at CCC. For the first time in a long time, I had a running project in front of me that filled me with awe and triggered my sportsmanlike ambition. I was stoked.

Well, this book is about a 100-mile run in the United States, not a 100-kilometer run in France. So, I will cut this short by just telling you that the CCC is a beautiful but also demanding mountain race that has shaped me as a runner in many ways. However, I crossed the finish line in Chamonix with completely neutral feelings. And I find that finishing emotion neither good nor bad, but, well, neutral.

I'm only guessing, but the reason my emotional amplitude stayed rather flat might have been because almost everything went according to plan. Apart from a few unexplainable energy dips that made me sit on a stone for a breather more often than I wanted, which I am not ashamed to mention here, I just about had a trouble-free race. Despite my short experience as an ultrarunner, I know that this is atypical for running such long distances. Even at shorter ultramarathons, such as 50-km or 50-mile races, you most likely face a good number of unexpected extra challenges and setbacks, as well as the often-related emotional highs and lows. That was not the case at my CCC, which left me with a nice, but not very intense, first 100-km race. The Levelhead was happy, though.

It was a rather brief journey from Chamonix to Olympic Valley. After a fit of spontaneous racing, including the Munich Marathon, the half-marathon distance at the Hochkönigman trail running festival just one week after CCC and the absolutely wonderful Limone Skyrace in Italy, I was sitting at our kitchen table with a couple of friends in early December 2021 when the Willpower Athletes group chat popped up on my phone:

"Chriiiissss!! You've won the lottery! They just announced your name!!"

Before I could properly realize what was going on, my inbox exploded with congratulations and good luck wishes for my upcoming "big race." This was the first real step in my Western States journey.

CHAPTER 2
ONE TICKET TO WESTERN STATES

" "You've got to ask yourself one question: 'Do I feel lucky?' Well, do you, punk?"

— DIRTY HARRY

With over 7,000 applications and only 360 entrants every year, the Western States Endurance Run has established itself as the most notorious lottery system in running. It's simple: if you run an official Western States qualifying race, usually a 100-kilometer or 100-mile distance, you earn one ticket to enter the lottery. Each year you qualify and apply again, the number of your lottery tickets doubles. After two years you got two tickets in, after three years four tickets, after four years eight tickets and so on. CCC was one of the qualifying races on the list, and I did what probably every ultrarunner in the world does — I threw my hat into the ring to get my ticket pile growing until in maybe five or six years I would be a lucky winner of the Western States lottery. I expected to keep running and training for a few years before getting in, gradually accumulating both ultramarathon fitness and tickets.

That's not what happened. Instead, I won the lottery with one ridiculous ticket in the first year I applied. That's right, *one* ticket. The odds that this happens are around 1.1%. On average, it takes a runner 7 years and 64 tickets in the lottery to have a reasonable 50% chance to get in. And even that is no guarantee. You bet I was quite surprised. *Shocked* would be a more accurate description of how I felt.

Let's dig a little deeper here, since the shock and surprise didn't evaporate any time soon. This key moment, and the emotions I felt in it, extend all the way to the very moment during Western States where I was absolutely convinced the race was over for me.

When I found out that I had won the Western States lottery, I felt a mix of awe, overwhelm, and embarrassment. I will explain the last feeling first. The simple but strict lottery system produces a huge number of runners who wait eagerly for years to get in — I personally know some of these runners. By qualifying each year they wait, they gain a constantly growing level of ultrarunning experience and an ever-growing hunger for the race. There are literally runners with 128 tickets in the lottery every year.

But it is a lottery, after all. And a lottery is always a matter of luck, at least in part. I had nothing to reproach myself for — I did nothing wrong. But I couldn't fully turn off the feeling that a more seasoned runner, who had been waiting longer, deserved the lottery win more than me. I felt I didn't belong on the Western States start line in Olympic Valley — at least, not yet.

The second impulse I felt was awe and overwhelm. It felt like I was being pushed into something that I didn't want to do, not yet. The challenge of running 100 miles — a distance I couldn't really grasp — in the mountains, in blistering heat, which I hate very much, really gave me goose bumps. And not the nice ones you get when your favorite song comes on or your spouse touches you gently. Rather, the cold ones that creep down your neck when you eat something gross or watch a horror movie.

Winning the Western States lottery does not mean you're automatically registered for the race. You can still turn down that opportunity. An oddity that does not happen as seldom as you might think. There are countless reasons to reject this once-in-a-lifetime offer: injury, training deficit, family obligations, travel restrictions, etc. Or simply a lack of confidence. That was me.

CHAPTER 3
DOUBTS AND DECISIONS

> "Fear is good. Like self-doubt, fear is an indicator. Fear tells us what we have to do."

— STEVEN PRESSFIELD, *THE WAR OF ART*

While my win of the lottery was some kind of accident, my final decision to run Western States was not. I was afraid. I was in doubt. I was hesitant. And I quarreled with myself. To solve this predicament, I decided to evaluate my strengths and weaknesses as a runner in general and ultrarunner in particular. The Levelhead ran to his favorite playground, a whiteboard, and scribbled a personal debit and credit list.

Reflecting upon my weaknesses was a sobering but also enlightening experience. Foremost, being extremely sensitive to heat is not particularly helpful when running Western States. The race is known for being one of the hottest in the world. The temperature in the canyons of the Sierra Nevada mountains usually rises to 104 °F (40 °C) and beyond. During hotter years, the dropout rate can be as high as 45%. Likewise, moving from a 100-km race distance to a 100-miler within less than a year would carry some risks and uncertainties. Those additional 40 miles make a difference to your body and mind. It takes years, if not decades, to become a truly experienced ultrarunner. I also reflected on the underlying "too much too soon" attitude that this project would imply. Or to put it into the words of my friend and former coach Martin Grüning: "There's not much left after Western States." I clearly understood what he meant by that. Although there are always races with longer distances, more altitude gain, or more difficult terrain, the truly iconic ultramarathons can be counted on one hand. Once you checked them off your list, there might be no desirable goals left. I figured I'd have to deal with that risk once this running project was over.

On the positive side, I also realized that I brought some helpful skills to the table. I am generally comfortable running at night. I also seem to have few issues with GI stress. This means I can usually eat all through a race without throwing up, which is a great asset. In fact, it's the most decisive skill in ultrarunning, next to being fit. I'm also a better downhill runner than a climber. Since Western States is a relative downhill course with more elevation loss than gain, I was mildly optimistic that my quad muscles wouldn't be shot too early in the race. Finally, I would label myself a good problem solver. Maybe not as much during the race, but definitely beforehand, while preparing mentally and strategically (see the chart below). I am good at creating game plans for all sorts of scenarios and if I'm lucky, one of these difficulties appears during a race instead of one of the million issues I don't have a game plan for.

Original Debit and Credit List for Western States

WHAT I'M ALREADY GOOD AT	WHAT I NEED TO WORK ON
Fueling usually goes very well during ultras. I know what I can eat while running, and I can eat a lot of it.	Heat resilience. Since I've been a runner, my performance is getting worse, starting from 25 °C (about 76° to 77 °F) and can fully shut down at above 30 °C. I really need to work on this for Western States.
I seem to have very little problems running at or through the night.	Overall endurance. Judging from the approximately 10 ultras I did, ranging from 50 km to 100 km, I would not say that I am ready to run a 100-miler regarding my overall endurance. Not yet.
My legs are much better prepared for running downhill than uphill.	Strength. I am very convinced that I need to level up on both leg and core strength for a 100-mile race in particular and as a runner in general.
I have a very well reflected and documented 100-km race that I can draw a lot from. Although it's only one 100 km race, it's still a big pool of knowledge.	Self-confidence. Other than with CCC, I do not have an unreserved *"yes, I think I can do this"* feeling for Western States. The challenge just seems too big right now to grasp it. It will hopefully change during training and most likely with the help of at least one serious preparation race.
I take things seriously and manage to regard such endeavors not just as "a race" but rather as a "life-project." Thus, I am willing and able to invest a lot of time and work to make it a great experience in the end.	
I will have a highly reliable and very motived crew and pacer(s) by my side.	
I have constant and full access to mountain terrain to train on. It's only a 50-minute drive or train ride and I can go there any time, even during the week.	
I am very flexible time-wise. I can take single days off any time and go on shorter and longer vacations for training.	

Original Debit and Credit List for Western States

None of the above was a guarantee that Western States would be a great race for me, or even that I would finish. On the other hand, none of the above doomed this project to fail.

While the Levelhead was handling this whole issue like a business decision, I was ignoring something. Something quiet, deep down inside of me: I **wanted** to run Western States. From the bottom of my heart. The Punk just wanted to do it. Go out there, run like hell, and see where it gets me. It was the Punk's typical childlike, almost naive curiosity, and exuberant optimism that it will be great. But I was too busy pushing the pros and cons around in my head to recognize this. Being a tiny bit more in touch with the Punk inside of me would have made things much easier. Not only to wrap up the pending race registration, but also handling the deep valley I would emotionally wander on race day.

Finally, it was my coach, Karim Ramadan, who tipped the scale. He convincingly laid out a smart and effective seven-month training plan that would not only prepare me to run 100 miles, but also looked very doable. Karim sowed an aura of great optimism and rock-hard confidence. He had a plan. And he believed in it. It was a well-balanced mix of consistent, almost stoical, endurance training, occasional speedwork, many long days in the mountains, and adequate rest, as well as some mental skills that would help me during tough workouts and even more so on race day. Karim convinced me that I would be fit and ready to run Western States. I trusted him and never regretted it. This was the moment a decision was made.

CHAPTER 4
MEETING THE COACH

 "Hills are the shortcut to success."

— ARTHUR LYDIARD

've known Karim since early 2021 when we've worked together on some mental aspects of my last marathon preparation. That was complemented by four weeks of physical coaching for my CCC race. The last four weeks, to be precise. I was late in bringing him to the game, but he did a great job managing the most critical phase before the big day.

But why work with a coach at all? For me, it provides consistency and structure. During such long preparation phases, I easily get lost. I tend to focus on the odds and ends of a training week and attach too much importance to single workouts instead of the big picture. If a workout doesn't go as expected, I often believe the whole preparation is in danger. It can be things like an increased heart rate, not hitting the right pace, or generally feeling weak during a run. This sometimes makes me want to trash the entire plan and compensate for a bad workout the day after. When someone else takes care of planning my training, I have a great sense of relief and it typically boosts my motivation. The second reason why working with a coach makes sense to me is expertise. When I invest a lot of time and energy into a long-term running project, I want to learn and evolve. Both physically and mentally. At the same time, I wish to run, not study.

Karim is a sports psychologist, but also an experienced and well-rounded physical coach for all sorts of endurance sports, especially ultra and mountain running. I first heard about Karim when he was featured on *Koop Cast*, one of my favorite running podcasts, hosted by ultrarunning coaching legend Jason Koop. Karim was invited to *Koop Cast* twice, discussing the topics of mental skills and self-talk for endurance athletes. Listening to his insights on the mental challenges of our sport piqued my interest. Shortly after his first *Koop Cast* appearance, I reached out via email and proposed the idea of him becoming my coach, a proposition he fortunately accepted.

I really like Karim's open-minded yet still scientific approach. He's among the new breed of coaches who are very well-connected and up to date with the latest papers on training theory, nutrition, sports psychology, and sports science in general. Karim does not make a great show of learning, though. Like me, he often follows a structured trial-and-error approach. If something works, he keeps it. If it doesn't work, he drops it and tries something new. Karim believes every athlete is different and there is no sole truth in training theory. He has a fresh and modern way of working with athletes from all sorts of backgrounds, and he emphasizes different aspects of training in each of his collaborations. After all, for Western States, it was great to have someone on my side who also addressed the mental aspects of running.

I must, however, admit that it took me some time to adapt to Karim's coaching style. In particular, he never shares a weekly or monthly workout overview with his athletes. Or at least not with me. I never asked him why that is. But over time, I found that it helps me to focus only on the next workout, instead of spending too much thought to upcoming runs that appear more important to me, such as *Sunday's long run* or *next week's hill repeats*. Therefore, a lot of seemingly unspectacular easy jogs, which I would have disparaged as junk miles in the past, gained my undivided attention. I learned to recognize their indispensable role within my training plan.

Karim seemed to be especially in love with one particular workout, though. It's called Rolling Hills. Usually between 1 and 2 hours, this medium-effort run is supposed to be done on profiled, yet runnable, terrain. The idea is to gain between 200 and 500 meters of altitude during the workout, without explicitly climbing steep ascents. I have no idea how many Rolling Hills I conquered during my Western States preparation, but it must have been dozens. Repeating one and the same workout stoically over weeks and months might sound odd at first glance, but once I started adapting to it, I found it a highly effective means to train and develop all three areas: endurance, strength, and tempo. True to Karim's motto: "If it works, do more of it."

I slowly but steadily kept on gaining both speed and endurance. Furthermore, Karim anticipated perfectly the particular running style I would need at Western States, especially during the last third of the race.

Moreover, Karim's profound questions about my thoughts and emotions regarding my training very often took me by surprise. One day, for example, he asked me to reflect on what a jog is to me while I was going out for a jog. Here's what I came up with for my blog:

> *A jog is to switch the watch face to clock mode. A jog is to be light on the feet. A jog is to not just listen to music, but to feel it. A jog is to briefly speed up to pass that old lady on a bike. A jog is to see, hear, and smell the surroundings. A jog is to deeply think everything through and then let it go. A jog is being excited for dinner, preparing the meal in your head. A jog is returning to your loved ones less exhausted and more full of energy. A jog is craving your next hard workout and recovering from past ones. A jog is a micro reset in life.*

Working with a coach who is also a sport psychologist is just different and occasionally a bit challenging. However, these fruitful discussions very regularly shed light into the darkness and pointed me in the right direction.

But one of the greatest qualities Karim brought to our coach-athlete-relationship was his composure. Whenever I freaked out about my stagnating athletic development or openly suspected my training was going nowhere, Karim remained calm. He listened closely to all my rants, but never hopped on my panic train. He didn't react at all to some of my whims, which pissed me off, but also encouraged me to reflect on myself. Almost without exception, I found out that I had gone overboard, and that things weren't as disastrous as I had expected. Surprise, surprise.

CHAPTER 5
THE COACH'S PLAYBOOK

 "If you have a body, you are an athlete."

— WILLIAM J. BOWERMAN

Karim brought a number of new training principles and philosophies into my running world. One of them was to balance the training load rather cautiously. Training for a big race is always a tightrope walk. If you do too little, you might not fully exploit your potential. If you do too much, you risk getting injured or burnt out. I often neglected this precautionary measure, especially in my early running years. With a lot of ambition and a general "more is better" attitude, I was constantly running the risk of overreaching and thereby compromising my training and racing results. It also occasionally spoiled the fun in running, and the sword of Damocles of injury was hovering above all the time. Fortunately, Karim got that well-balanced for me, with adequate rest between hard workouts and recurring rest weeks with significantly less training load.

In fact, in those seven months of my Western States preparation, I never had the feeling of being overtrained or burnt out. Not one single day. This included big training weeks and runcations with more than 18 hours of running on mountainous terrain. Karim and I had the following agreement:

> If you don't feel like running one day: no problem. If you don't feel like running two days in a row, cut the next workout by one quarter. If you don't feel like running three days in a row, take a day off immediately. You don't even have to tell me.

I never needed such a self-imposed emergency day off, but I got his point and kept track of my mood and energy levels.

Another new approach Karim's coaching introduced me to is a rather small, but highly effective one: paying attention to training hours instead of milage. As runners, we all have a personal threshold of what we call "a good training week." Usually, it's a number of workouts or, in my case, a certain number of kilometers per week that gives me that desirable feeling of accomplishment. For me and a lot of my fellow runners, it is 100 kilometers (ca. 62 miles). Switching the mindset to training hours instead of milage is a true game changer. It ends the embarrassing extra loop around your block to fulfill that extra kilometer. It prevents you from running stupid junk miles. Likewise, it adds pride to focused strength training and alternative sports and makes them real workouts instead of just annoying add-ons. But most of all, it converges your training to the realities of ultrarunning. For most of us, this sport is not about how fast you can run a mile, but rather how many hours you can stay on your feet and move forward.

Through Karim, I also learned to structure my training after my own RPE scale. RPE stands for Rating of Perceived Exertion, and it's a simple concept. You rate or plan your workouts by a scale of 1 to 10, where 1 is the easiest possible run and 10 is the absolute maximum effort you can deliver. Many coaches rely heavily on this subjective and non-technical measurement instead of objective data from heart rate monitors or power meters. Especially in ultrarunning, heart rate plays a subordinate role. It's just not very meaningful because of ever-changing terrain, heat, altitude, and phenomena like cardiac drift due to the length of the workouts and races. Power meters have come a long way, but also fail to deliver any helpful data in erratic environments like trails. RPE, in contrary, is simple and highly effective.

It can be a bit tricky to rate your perceived exertion precisely, though. While 1 and 10 seem somewhat clear, the difference between 6 and 7, for example, might not be so easy to tell. Where do you draw the line? If you look up RPE on Google, you will find a long list of helpful tables. Most of them put the different levels of perceived exertion in relation to intensity of breathing and ability to speak. Those guidelines do not really work for me, so I came up with my own personal RPE scale, which kind of goes like this:

1. I am running, but basically, it feels like going for a walk
2. A very easy effort that is not demanding at all
3. Flow-ish easy run on a comfortable level
4. Feels like working out, slightly uncomfortable but still very doable
5. Real running. This is how the first 15k of a marathon ideally feels like

6. Marathon effort. Feels fast and sustainable, but also demanding
7. Half-marathon effort. Right on the border of "Yes, I can do this" and "No, this is too fast"
8. Feels like racing a 10k minus the last 1–2 kilometers
9. Pushing maximal hard, trying to sustain an unsustainable pace
10. All-out final spurt level. Feels like blacking out without blacking out

Most other RPE scales I have seen do not include anything like my 10/10 effort, which isn't a training zone anyway. As an endurance athlete, you don't push yourself that hard often. However, I added it to my personal RPE scale to remind myself that there is always a level of "running harder" I haven't reached yet.

I also have forceful feelings about all RPE levels.

1-3: Any time. "Running, yeah!"

4-5: Everything from "This sucks so much. I am a terrible runner" to "I feel like flying! Which way to the Olympics?"

6: The magic effort. However, I need to avoid looking at my pace because I immediately convert it into a marathon time

7-8: I need to have a good reason to push that hard. A race, for example. Or the last rep of a 1,000 m or 2,000 m interval

9: This sucks very much, but it's part of the game

10: Interestingly, I find this less awful than a 9/10 effort. Probably because it usually only lasts a couple of seconds

For me, RPE has become a small but important daily reflection. It speaks to both the Punk and the Levelhead. On the one hand, it's a clear measure, but it's also very intuitional. RPE sharpens my awareness of what is actually going on while I'm running, where my current abilities are at and, most of all, how different the same workout can feel on any given day. After all, we're humans and not machines. Thank goodness.

CHAPTER 6
SET YOUR GOALS

 "What keeps me going is goals."

— MUHAMMAD ALI

The months of preparation gave me plenty of time to reflect on which concrete goal I wanted to reach between Olympic Valley, California, where Western States starts, and the finish in Auburn. Fortunately, the sport of ultrarunning makes this easy. Because of its lovable simplicity, the metrics are quite obvious: distance, time and altitude gain and loss, respectively. In most cases, distance and difference in elevation are set values by the race. This leaves most of us with a bare time goal for our running challenges.

While the Punk just shows up and runs, the Levelhead usually splits his race goals into A, B, and C categories. Instead of making a single objective my goal, I often have three objectives. This lets me expand my scope of action, especially when things don't go as planned. So if your most ambitious A-Goal slips into unreachable territory, I can easily switch to my still-challenging B-Goal, or even my still-satisfying C-Goal, if things keep on falling apart.

But Western States was different. After weeks of thinking it through, I came to realize that I actually had just one goal. I called it the ABC-Goal because it included everything I wished for regarding this race. I wanted to be an official Western States 100 finisher. Therefore, I had to reach the track at Placer High School in Auburn within a 30-hour time limit. That's all I wanted and all I needed to do. Nothing more, but also nothing less.

I was very aware that looking at my previous running achievements and my training log suggested that my goals for Western States could have been a bit more ambitious. But I simply didn't feel it. This doesn't mean I wasn't going to run these 100 miles as fast as I could. I would try to for sure. However, I was neither triggered nor motivated by any other time or placing goal. It just wasn't there. On the other hand, I also did not detect any nonchalant attitude like "I'm all in for the experience. If I drop out after 30 miles, I will still be happy and thankful" inside of me. Absolutely not. I wanted to finish Western States. And I wanted to do it in under 30 hours. Lo and behold, my ABC-Goal was set.

Let me throw in a little side story here. Ever since I ran my first fast-ish road marathon in 2018, basically everyone I knew assumed I could easily run a sub-3-hour marathon as well. They not only assumed, but almost expected me to do it. In their mind, it was a total no-brainer. Well, it's 2023, and I still have a 3:03 hour PB, solid as a rock. What I am trying to say is that extrapolating previous race and training results only goes so far, especially if you are speculating about a race or racing distance you have never done before. That's why I refrained from projections like these a long time ago, and I'm doing quite well with it until this day. Western States became an excellent demonstration why this rule makes sense. At least for me.

CHAPTER 7
CONSISTENCY AND COMMITMENT

 "Consistency is key."

— KARIM RAMADAN (AND OTHERS)

truly love training plans. Yes, I do. I know that for many people, structured training is solely a means to an end, something they have to do to become a better runner. It's an annoying duty that is to be mastered so that they can peak and shine on race day. There are also numerous runners who claim not to train at all. At least not in a structured way, such as with a fixed schedule. They simply hate it that much. Of course, there are also people who cannot afford the necessary time investment because other things in their life are much more important.

And then there are people like me: training nerds, schedule enthusiasts, the pedants of running. When I have a training plan, I just feel disentangled. It gives me a feeling of safety and calm. It literally structures my life. It delivers order, a state I am trying to acquire constantly and have been since I was a teenager, long before I even knew what a training plan was. It's a means of letting go and just doing something for the sake of doing it. Finding meaning in seemingly meaningless actions. Even a bit of the much-quoted "living in the present moment." Like this:

Q: "Why are you going out for a 35k run? It's raining."
A: "Because it's on the plan."

There's always a good chance that such runs, that normally would have been skipped, turn out to be wonderful.

The other big advantage of training on a fixed schedule is that I can have a significant number of micro successes. Each session, especially if it's a tough one, has the potential to leave me with elation and great contentment. On the other hand, failed workouts can easily be left behind without much mental or physical damage. The balance can be really gratifying, as long a training plan is not overstraining or demanding too little.

A training routine is also an endless pool of wisdom. Like one big field experiment. Every single training session is affected by other aspects of life and running. What did I eat? And when? How many hours of sleep did I get? How stressful was my day? Is there anything that concerns me? Which shoes did I pick? What was on my headphones? Did I use the foam roller the night before or not? How was the weather? Did meditation calm my mind or make me sleepy? Was there a difference between running alone or with someone else? The list continues forever. While on race day all of this is a one-shot, you can easily go wild on trial-and-erroring in training. A method that has been my true friend forever.

Yes, this is the Levelhead speaking here. Structured and well-thought-out plans are his favorite playground. And you know what? During such a long-term preparation, it makes perfect sense to keep a cool head and just get the job done. However, at the end of the day, I am very aware that training only gets you so far. Races are won, and ambitious goals are reached with the help of some other driving force that can not be trained or prepared for in the same way. At least not with pace and mileage. However, the year has 300 training days, more or less, and only a handful of race days. A good reason to give your training some love.

With this in mind, I scrupulously documented my seven months of preparation for the Western States Endurance Run. The things that I paid most attention to when journaling every week were much less tangible than sheer numbers. It was more about why I'd run and what I'd learned.

Weekly Training Reflections

WEEK	MOTTO	WHAT I LEARNED	BEST WORKOUT
01	Painfully Slow	You have to let go if you want a fresh start	"Rolling Hills with Rolling People" (17 km / 1:32 h / 174 m D+)
02	Keep rolling rolling...	There's not much to lose in running. Except for toenails and speed	"Rolling Hills Have Eyes" (12 km / 1:08 h / 308 m D+)
03	The mountain won't let me go	Consistency is key	"Long run with a View" (26 km / 2:30 h / 806 m D+)
04	Rolling F*cking Hills	If you don't feel like running one day: no problem. If you don't feel like running two days in a row: cut the next workout by 1/4. If you don't feel like running 3 days in a row: take a day off immediately	"Rolling Hills Rolling Hills Rolling Hills" (17 km / 1:20 h / 247 m D+)
05	Big Weeks, Big Fun	Bad workouts make the good ones greater	Back-to-back-to-back long run weekend (63 km / 5:30 h / 462 m D+)
06	Can you do the same again?	Adaption happens when you bend but do not break	Triple back-to-back long-run weekend XL (61 km / 5:32 h / 988 m D+)
07	Take a good rest	Overtraining is a thing. Overresting is not	Short-ish Rolling Hills on a 5/10 effort (16 km / 1:10 h / 243 m D+)
08	Everything will work for Western States. Literally, everything	Let's fix it before it becomes a real problem	I wish it would have been my *"Do What You Want"* 6/10 Tempo Run, but it was terrible. No faves this week
09	Repetition yields great results	Base training is a foundation you can literally build everything upon	Unofficial New Year's 10k race (one minute slower than PB, two minutes faster than expected)

Weekly Training Reflections Part 1

10	How are you feeling in general?	Running fast makes you feel fast. Even if you don't run fast	"Rolling Hills Longrun" with Michi (30 km / 2:30 h / 400 m D+)
11	We will take it to the next level over the coming weeks	Does it contribute to my goal? Yes: keep it. No: change it	No highlight this week
12	Can you do a very long run on Wednesday?	Overanalyzing is the death of trusting the process	Both best and worst workout was the "Wednesday Longrun" (42 km / 3:38 h / 248 m D+)
13	Cruise along, test nutrition and try not to sit on a stone	It's not about the race. It's about the people	Starnberger See Ultra (49 km / 4:12 h / 321 m D+)
14	You will go for the fun	Peak shape is a goal. Not a status quo	Parkrun Westpark (5 km / 18:44 min+32 m D+)
15	Ditch the poles & control your effort, even if you feel well	It takes time to build endurance. In comparison, getting faster is a low-hanging fruit	Runcation Day 4 from Sao Vicente to Ribeira Granda (21km /2:25 h / 1066 m D+)
16	It's impressive that you feel fresh	No progress without struggle	Maybe the best workout since I started training for Western States. "50 min 5/10 effort" with a surprisingly fast and easy feeling pace of 4:09 min/km. Right after a massive week in the mountains with 142 km and 8000 m D+
17	Of course, there will be a long run: 43k (ca. 26 miles) is a little too long though	I can run with hand bottles	"Rolling Hills in actual hills" (17 km / 1:51 h / 524 m D+)
18	Repeat yesterday as it was	Running faster means more kilometers in less time. Magic!	"5/10 effort on flat" (14 k / 1:00 h / 60 m D+)
19	Make a plan. And then stick to it	How to find meaning in seemingly meaningless actions	Kandel Marathon (5 km warm up / 30 km fast / 7 km cool down / 3:10 h)

Weekly Training Reflections Part 2

20	2 long runs, but not insanely long	How to surprise yourself by feel	"5/10 effort on flat" (17 km / 1:10 h / 71 m D+)
21	Looking forward to seeing how results will be in a few months	"Let the race come to you." And if it doesn't show up, just enjoy the ride	Temporun at Lindkogel Trail (21 km / 2:05 h / 1100 m D+)
22	Elevation gain is what we need	When it snows, it pours	"Longrun w/ Gains" with the crew (22 km / 2:21 h / 871 m D+)
23	Enjoy the mountains	Trust. It's all about trust	2x 20 min up the Wank (14 km / 1:46 h / 1075 m D+)
24	Are you excited?	There is no right or wrong reason to run a race	"Wedding Oly" (6.6 km / 0:37 h / 74 m D+)
25	Oh, no! I wanted you to go and enjoy your capacity at the Madeira Ultra Trail (MIUT)	After all, it's about something much bigger than Western States. It's about being healthy and able to run at all	COVID-19. No Workouts
26	You will need a few more days to be back to normal	I have made peace with possibly not being in peak shape, but running Western States must be medically justifiable	"Phasing in VI" Rolling Hills (15 km / 1:22 h / 426 m D+)
27	You will peak perform at the right time, you'll see	Small steps are still steps	"Phasing in XI" IATF Support Run (25.7 km / 2:46 h / 860 m D+)
28	Let's work with what we've got	I can't run hard and fast anymore. For Western States I need to run long and smoothly, though	"Easy Mountain Longrun /-Hike" up to Scharnitzjoch (20 km / 3:00 h / 1227 m D+)
29	Reinforce recovery	How to negotiate with the heat	"The real mountains" Feldernjöchl from Ehrwald with Emi and Lisa (16 km / 2:03 h / 1093 m D+)
30	Unleash yourself	The goal is to run Western States. Everything else is irrelevant	"Let the race come to you" Ursa Trail Half-Marathon (21 km / 2:17 h / 1095 m D+)

Weekly Training Reflections Part 3

31	Everything pays into WSER	Bring more snacks!	Unofficial Speed Trail at Hochkönigman race w/ Lisa (21 km / 2:19 h / 1160 m D+)
32	Basically everything we did in training combined in one week	If it works, do more of it	Triple Back-To-Back Weekend (60 km / 8:23 h / 2800 m D+ / 3800 m D-)
33	Connecting	Running is about bonding with other people, and I have the best friends in the world	Escarpment & High Country Longrun (19 km / 2:30 h / 1128 m D+)
34	It's going to be a different race experience	Ultras are run with the heart, not the head	*Western States 100*

Weekly Training Reflections Part 4

CHAPTER 8
VISUALIZING FAILURE

66 "When I get there, I've already pictured what's going to happen a million times so I don't actually have to think about it."

— MISSY FRANKLIN

When I was not running, I stood in front of a whiteboard to plan my race. I am a very visual person. When I have an image of something in my head, it's much easier for me to deal with it. That's why I started creating so-called "race scripts" last year. That's basically a visualization of the most important characteristics of a race. The first event I did this for was CCC, my first 100-km ultramarathon. Being a whiteboard nerd, I took to this task like a duck to water. Besides a detailed elevation profile, markers for aid stations, names of mountains and villages, crew meeting points, cutoff times, sunrise and sunset info, and occasional notes on my racing strategy, I also browsed the internet for photos of significant sections or crucial spots on the racecourse. I find this particularly helpful if it's the first time I'm running a certain race and have no idea what to expect. It all adds up to a wonderful race script whiteboard scribble that slowly consolidates into a picture of me running on race day. To memorize all the details, I go through the script several times and try to imagine running along the course, experiencing all the details I've laid out. Since my CCC race script stood the test, I did the exact same thing for Western States as well.

But Karim brought this method to a higher level with the following advice: "Don't visualize perfection. Visualize failure and manipulate it!"

In practice, this means not picturing myself running the course on a beautiful day, feeling strong from start to finish and having no troubles whatsoever. Instead, I imagine myself in the pouring rain, twisting my ankle, completely running out of energy, dehydrated, falling over, having a massive headache, throwing up everything I eat, and freezing terribly. Then I visualize how I would resolve these problems during the race. Here are some of my Western States scenarios:

"On the climb up to Robinson Flat, you fall over and graze your knee. What do you do about it?"

"When passing Deadwood Canyon you run out of water with no aid station coming soon. How do you handle this?"

"You're running in the High Country and find your rhythm, but your shoelaces keep on untying themselves until you finally trip over them and fall. What now?"

You get the idea. If you repeat this exercise a couple of times, you get a more realistic picture of what racing a particular course will be like. You will also produce a solid game plan for a good number of things that can and will go wrong on race day.

Creating the race script for Western States was both great fun and terrifying. Mainly because I would have to deal with some challenges that were entirely new to me. Most notably, I had never raced 100 miles before, and I had never raced in such intense heat. Both of these Western States prime features scared the hell out of me. However, I was certain that in the end it was going to be like all other ultramarathons: the number of things that can go wrong and get you into trouble is endless. And whatever is going to eat you alive will most likely not be what you have prepared yourself for. Turns out, I was very right about this.

Still, I was adamant and consistent in girding myself for whatever Western States would throw at me. My training unfolded beautifully, but doubts were my constant companion.

CHAPTER 9
ENJOYING THE PROCESS

> "If there is one rule, an unbreakable rule, it's that patience is necessary for greatness."
>
> — RICK RUBIN

During my 34 weeks of preparation, I never felt like I trained really hard. My coach, Karim, is a staunch believer of proper recovery, and it looks like he's right about that. No one can train solely peak weeks for over half a year. There's gotta be time for rest. Time to let the body and mind heal. Time to ease the stress and find new strength. This absolutely makes sense to me. The more emotional part of my brain spoke a different language, though.

"You could have done more!"

"Where's your vert? Are you training in the mountains at all?"

"Those 100k weeks... you need to do more of those!"

"Did you even strength train?"

"Where's that VO$_2$max at now?"

I also often asked myself the following key question: "What do I get for the work I put into training?"

Well, for the most part, running itself is the reward. And that's an honest answer. Simply being outside, being able to run far and fast, and most of all, able to run at all, is a great gift that I truly appreciate.

However, there were days during my Western States preparation when I just went through the motions to reach my ABC-Goal. But just doing the job is precisely how consistent training works. Doubts were always present, though. I never knew for sure if a certain workout or training phase would pay off as I hoped. There simply is no visible "run-o-meter" that adds another "endurance point" to my "training bank account." Of course, there are tools, but they can only interpret the tip of the training iceberg and its effect on your body and mind. So, no VO$_2$max, no Suffer Score, no TSS or CTL can guarantee you reach your goals in the end.

Of course, I knew that training had an effect. The rule of stress and adaptation universally applies to every athlete, and so far, there hasn't been one single year in my running career in which I did not profit from that. Looking back on where you have started and where you are today is a mighty source of inspiration and also motivation to keep on following this path. But for me, it did not kill the entirety of my doubts about whether this progression would be enough to run 100 miles through the mountains.

Bottom line: training is a bit like truly loving someone. Only if your love is unconditional, without the expectation of any tangible and immediate return, can it fully unfold.

"Trust the process": that's what they say. And they are right. Once, I even read "Enjoy the process." This is even more right. And that's what I tried to do throughout my training until I stood on the start line in Olympic Valley. Along the way, I had run 1,615 miles (ca. 2,600 km) with 192.913 feet (ca. 58,800 m) of vertical gain and loss. Much more meaningful, at least to the *Levelhead*, was the number 288, though. That's how many hours I've run during my seven-month Western States preparation. As stated earlier in this book, these are just numbers. They were just half the battle on my way to Auburn. Maybe even less than half.

However, I took my preparation to reach my ABC-Goal very seriously. That's why I went on vacation. Sort of.

CHAPTER 10
RUNCATION IS THE NEW VACATION

 "Run. Eat. Sleep. Repeat."

— UNKNOWN

My Western States preparation included not one, but two so-called *runcations*. A runcation combines a vacation and a training camp, trying to merge the best of two worlds. Ideally, you end up doing nothing but running, eating, and relaxing. Truly a dream life, if you ask me. The two runcations added great value to my race preparation and also mental well-being. I used my annual leave for both runcations, so they were truly time off my busy everyday life.

My first runcation was in February 2022 and led Lisa and me to Madeira, a wonderful Portuguese island in the Atlantic Ocean. We chose Madeira because of its warm climate, massive climbs, and breathtaking flora. But it was also a course check for what was planned to be my only Western

States preparation race: the Madeira Ultra Trail (MIUT) in April, about 2.5 months before Western States. We managed to cover considerable parts of its epic route. Other than that, Madeira is a very relaxed and laid-back island if you stay out of its capital, Funchal. We loved the vibes.

Lisa, who is also an ultrarunner, and I went out on the MIUT racecourse for eight days in a row with just one day off, which, not entirely coincidentally, was my forty-third birthday. On every run, we were impressed by the overwhelming diversity of the trails. We ran on bumpy dirt roads, tiny paths carved into stone walls, thick jungles, small villages, dark forests, countless tunnels and caves, along sandy beaches and on rocky stairways at high altitude. Right on the first day, Lisa and I lost all touch with time and distance and ran the complete last part of the MIUT racecourse backward, from Machico to Poiso. We were so excited about the beauty of the island that we totally forgot that there is no public transport, and we had to run all the way back to where we started. After a long day, we ended up with a 50 km (ca. 31 miles) run and 2,000 meters of altitude gain. Tired but blessed, we both ate three plates of pasta and contently fell into bed. A thoroughly worthy prelude for our runcation.

While discovering further parts of the MIUT racecourse, we particularly enjoyed the area around Pico Grande. It's the middle part of the MIUT route, shortly before the biggest climb up to Pico Ruivo. The rolling terrain from Encumeada up to the top and the beautiful downhill to Curral Das Freiras were just breathtaking, an unadulterated mix of winding dirt and rock paths, massive stone walls and densely covered, jungle-like forests. The scenery was changing completely every few kilometers, and we were continually amazed. What a wonderful place.

Regarding my Western States preparation, this runcation gave me confidence that the many foundational workouts and rolling hills I did during the past three months made sense. Although I felt like I was getting slower and slower, I had obviously built a solid endurance base. On Madeira, I could finally put it to use. My body handled the large mileage and altitude gains with ease, and I felt stronger with every day. I surely didn't push too hard on those runs and found the perfect balance of being maxed out but not empty at the end of each day.

But what struck me the most about our runcation on Madeira was that I did not think once about time, distance, or altitude. I just ran. A lot. My coach gave me all the freedom to do so. Breaking free from the routine training schedule for one week was a smart move and made the Punk rejoice.

In retrospect, traveling to Madeira to train definitely was one of the core components of my Western States preparation. My second runcation turned out to be a completely different experience, as my preparation had come to an abrupt standstill.

CHAPTER 11
THE PLAGUE, ACT I

> "You have power over your mind — not outside events. Realize this, and you will find strength."
>
> — MARCUS AURELIUS

In April 2022, I got a COVID-19 infection and my running was pretty much derailed. After one week of acute symptoms and no running at all, I was at first very hopeful when I slowly picked it up again. I started from scratch, increased volumes cautiously, and generally felt good while running with no coughing or headache. My body, especially my lungs and my heart, were speaking a different language, though. No matter how easy the effort, my heart rate was up by 20 beats. Even if you don't care much about heart rate during training, that's a lot. My slowest pace felt like a tempo run, and when I pushed harder, my heart and lungs felt as if they were about to explode. I played around with more rest, longer and shorter, faster and slower workouts, but this condition remained unchanged for the following five weeks.

Needless to say, my Western States preparation could not go on as planned. Yes, I was running. Yes, I was doing okay volumes. No, this was not a structured training schedule as it should have been for a 100-mile race. Worst of all, I had to cancel my only big preparation race, the Madeira Ultra Trail. This was not only unbelievably sad, but also a major stumbling block in my training. Race events are perfect to test nutrition, practice aid station routines, work on your pacing, learning to deal with heat under stress and, most of all, being on your feet for a long day. But even more, they give you the confidence, albeit no guarantee, that it is, in fact, possible to run 100 miles. The Levelhead was not amused about this deviation from the plan.

Recovery proceeded slowly. However, I had made peace with not being in peak shape on that starting line in Olympic Valley. I was even contemplating that I might not start at all, or that I might start but not be able to finish. One part of me was very frustrated that I had been thrown back so badly in the most critical phase of my preparation. Another, more rational, part of me was much more humble and relaxed. First, the timing could have been much worse. A COVID-19 infection shortly before hopping on a plane, or, even more horrific, when in the US, would immediately kill any chance of running Western States at all. Second: when talking to other COVID-19 afflicted runners, I witnessed a broad spectrum of healing processes. From: "After 10 days, everything was back to normal" to "I've been struggling to get out of bed for over a year now. Running is completely out of reach for me."

I realize that I was somewhere in the middle of how hard long- and post-COVID symptoms can hit you. Therefore, I was genuinely thankful.

For weeks, I ended up taking my training day-to-day. But ultimately, it was another runcation that finally untangled the threads.

CHAPTER 12
RUNCATION COMEBACK

66 "Let's work with what we've got."

— KARIM RAMADAN

This was the motto that Karim and I agreed on as I pitched a tent for my second runcation, in Litochoro, on the foot of Mount Olympus in Greece. Why go to Greece? There were three reasons. First, it's almost as hot as the canyons of the Sierra Nevada Mountains. At least that's what I thought. Even in May, temperatures climb to 32 °C (ca. 90 °F). That was adequate heat training and would help me to adapt to the most difficult challenge of Western States. Second, there are endless trail running options in Greece. From forest paths over infinite climbs up to 3,000 meters, to high altitude stone deserts, you get it all. Third, I could meet with Karim, who lives there and whom I hadn't seen since last year's CCC. Long story short, I was glad to be in Greece.

This time I traveled alone, without Lisa, the best running partner in the world. Unfortunately, she didn't have enough holiday left to join me. After all, we would be flying to California very soon, and we had also settled our trip to Chamonix for her own A-Race, the CCC at UTMB. But, despite these plausible reasons, I missed her terribly.

Running around Mount Olympus compensated me well, though. Rising to 2,917 meters (ca. 9,570 ft), it is one of the highest peaks in Europe, regarding its topographic prominence. The Greek mythology vibe is omnipresent, and the flora is exceptionally diverse. The upper part was still covered in snow, so running became quite adventurous from time to time. But at the end of each day I went to bed in Litochoro with a remarkable sunset view in the face of Mytikas, the highest peak in the area, right in front of me. A truly inspiring place to be.

After playing around at Mount Olympus for five days, I moved on to a town called Metsovo for the weekend, to do an event called Ursa Trail. I participated in all three races: a vertical K on Friday, a marathon on Saturday, and a half-marathon on Sunday. It was Karim's idea to give my runcation a special touch with this triple effort. I hadn't raced in a while, so I was excited.

The first event in the lovely Ursa Trail was the Katara Vertical K, a distance of 4.7 km and an altitude gain of 860 meters. Karim gave me the green light to go all-out. Because of this, but also because I only raced a vertical once in my fragmentary racing career, I was actually a bit nervous. The last thing he said to me before the race was: "Unleash yourself."

And I did.

The Katara Vertical really deserves its name. It's an 18%-ish climb, with literally not one single flat or downhill meter. It's just one massive uphill through woods, gravel roads, stone meadows, singletrail, and 100 meters of asphalt just before the finish line. The heat and the steepness hit hard right after the first couple of minutes. I could intensely feel myself throughout the race, and I realized that I had missed that a lot.

Funny side note with a deep edge: there was absolutely no information about this race or its results on the internet. I had no idea if I came in 10th or 100th. In fact, I don't even know how many other participants started. I had absolutely zero chance to compare myself to other runners, which usually happens automatically, even to a not-so-competitive runner like me. Yet still, I was very satisfied with how things went for me personally. And that's why I race.

Due to the wild mix of training fatigue, the heat, poor sleep, and the very different characteristics of my workouts, I really didn't know where I stood regarding my post-COVID symptoms. I still noticed some irregularities, like my heart rate being capped slightly above my lactate threshold while my breathing frequency was at the absolute maximum, and my legs felt almost fresh when I crossed the finish line. Sorry for the technical jargon. What was most important: I wasn't worried about any of it, and I started caring less and less.

The next day was an ultra day. In fact, the Ursa Trail Marathon, despite its name, was not an ultra or even a marathon because it only featured 40 km and 2,800 meters of elevation gain. Nonetheless, the plan was to kind of simulate what I planned to do at Western States. To some extent, it worked. I ran the first half a little too fast, but then was rudely thwarted by some very steep climbs. I mean *very* steep, the kind of steep where someone has attached an iron chain to parts of the trail as a climbing aid. You'd normally suspect this kind of climb to lurk in alpine terrain, not on the gently rolling trails of Greece. The racecourse had a lot more of surprises like this up its sleeve and thus never got boring. However, in the second half, I really found my rhythm, a sustainable ultra shuffle that probably didn't look very athletic. But using it, I felt I could continue for a long time and even have fun along the way. And that was precisely what I needed for Western States.

The last day of my runcation and the third race at Ursa Trail was a seemingly manageable 21 km race with 1,100 meters of altitude gain. But when I woke up the morning after the marathon from a terrible night of sleep, I didn't feel like racing at all. I would rather have enjoyed a freddo espresso and watched the race as a spectator. Hoping that my dizziness and fatigue would disappear at some point on the trail, I ran the first 5 kilometers very conservatively and just tried to enjoy the ride.

Halfway through the first climb, I recognized my legs were surprisingly fresh. I had recently started to practice the mental skill of focusing on the body parts that were working well instead of those with the aches and pains. So, I made use of my fresh legs and encouraged myself to run long stretches of the climb instead of hiking them. I passed a good dozen runners, and the race was on. I managed to run the second half progressively ever faster, opening up my stride in the downhills, rolling in the flats, and running most of the uphills. The last 2 kilometers into town were pure bliss and tangible love for running. Everything in life made sense.

And what about those post-COVID symptoms? Later in the evening, I found out that my heart rate monitor hadn't worked. During the past five weeks, I had been checking my heart rate immediately after every run to look for abnormalities and bad news. That I unconsciously didn't do that right after the race made me happy. COVID-19 still might have been somewhere in my body, but much less in my head anymore.

Eight runs, three races, 130 kilometers, 8,692 meters of altitude gain and 18:43 hours of running: those are the hard facts of my Greek runcation. I got some real quality workouts into my legs, trained my heat adaption, and tested my pacing and fueling strategies. All for the big race 26 days later. But what's most outstanding is how this runcation had changed my mindset toward Western States. After my COVID-19 infection, I struggled with anger, frustration, and self-doubt for weeks. Seven days of nothing but running rebuilt my self-confidence bit by bit and made me much more at ease. Basically with everything, but most of all with myself. It was the right decision to take the time off and travel to Greece. And even more to let the Punk do the running, not the Levelhead.

There wouldn't have been a better place for my runcation. The running culture in Greece is absolutely vibrant. I was so glad I had stepped out of my Germany-Austria-Switzerland-Italy-France bubble and learned about the social meaning of running in a country I didn't have on my radar until then. Running in Greece is very competitive. There's surely a lot of pressure, especially on the top athletes. But on the other hand, running truly unites people over there. Everyone is very much into the essence of this sport and there's great support for each other. Moreover, the races are very well organized and have exciting, beautiful courses. So next time you plan to run up the same old dirt road at Zugspitz Ultratrail for the 100th time (or whatever your local race is), you might consider racing in Greece instead.

The remaining weeks before my trip to the USA went by fast, and running was more or less pushed into the background by travel arrangements and organizational tasks. Either way, things were getting serious now, and Western States was about to become reality. And not just for me as a participant, but also for the lovely travel party who accompanied me.

CHAPTER 13
THE CREW IS ME, THE CREW IS YOU

66 "Yeah, we're the crew!"

— 7 SECONDS, *THE CREW*

E very adventure is only half the fun if you experience it alone. So I was more than happy to bring a couple of close friends to California. They would not only observe my first 100-mile race, but also support me with all their smartness, experience, organizational talent, medical knowledge, humor, cooking skills, muscle strength and endurance. And they have a lot thereof. Please meet my Western States travel party.

Henning and I have a lot in common, although he is the significantly better runner. We share the same kind of humor, which is actually not funny (only our wives think so). He's also very self-assured and convincing when he is technically wrong. But it's not what you say, but how you say it, right? We're both going places with this handy soft skill. One thing we don't have in common is that I have run Western States by the time I write this book, and he's still fervently dreaming of it. I never told him this, but he is one of the runners I had in mind when I felt a bit embarrassed to win the Western States lottery with just one ticket. I will definitely be there when it's his turn. And this will happen soon. I can feel it.

I also share some common character traits with his wife, **Christiane**. We're both too top-heavy at times. Especially when racing. Sometimes it's easier to switch off your brain and just go wild. This certainly doesn't make us less passionate runners and yes, we're both working on it.

Both Henning and Christiane had already been at Western States in 2019, crewing and pacing their friend Josef on his journey to an impressive 23:09:32-hour finish. Their previous experience and profound knowledge were of inestimable value for my own shot at this epic race. Their job was to keep an eye on timing and transport.

Not many runners bring their own medic to their race. With **Marie,** I was lucky enough to do so. Actually, she's an anesthesiologist. Not particularly helpful, when you're already knocked out by fatigue, but she was also prepared to treat my blisters, patch up minor and major cuts and sprains, and examine my overall physical condition. Furthermore, she got the job of tracking my carb and fluid intake during the race. Marie is also a dedicated runner, still rather at the beginning of her running career. I am mentioning her rookie status here because it is wonderful to see how much joy and fulfillment she finds in all the first-time races she's working through right now. I'm not so much ahead of her, but I thoroughly enjoy the experience every time I am present at such a memorable race.

Michi is cool as a cucumber. At least that's his aura when you run by his side. This, in addition to his truly amiable nature, makes him the perfect pacer, and that's the job he was assigned. Maybe I should rather call it an honor instead of a job. As a pacer, you can run the best part of Western States without the fear of being barbecued somewhere in a canyon. Michi's love for running is unbreakable, and he regularly embarks on challenging running projects himself.

Last, but definitely not least, there was **Lisa.** I still get goose bumps when I say or write this: *my wife.* We got married in April 2022, and I can forthright say that she is the love of my life. In addition to the most wonderful human being, I also married one of the most experienced ultrarunners I know. Lisa has finished and won races that I wouldn't even dare to sign up for. Her style of racing is pure fervor. She runs with all her heart and regularly grows far beyond herself if she gets carried away. I made her the crew captain of my Western States adventure, and could not think of anyone more fitting for that job.

That's it. My friends and family were my crew and pacers. Can anything better happen to a runner? I guess not. I felt grateful and honored to be accompanied by such a great bunch of people.

CHAPTER 14
CALIFORNIA BOUND

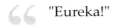 "Eureka!"

— CALIFORNIA STATE MOTTO

Hello, America. After a not-so-terrible flight to San Francisco, we arrived 10 days before the great day to have enough time to acclimatize to the heat and altitude. Western States starts at about 6,200 feet (ca. 1,890 m), goes up to 8,750 (ca. 2,667 m) and stays roughly above 7,000 feet (ca. 2,134 m) for almost the complete first third of the race. Our early arrival also gave us the chance to get rid of the annoying jet lag. After all, we now were nine hours ahead of German time, and it really messed up our circadian rhythms.

Traveling to the United States of America is always special to me. I went there for the first time at the age of 16 and remained fascinated by the immense contradictions of the country every time I came back. Inconceivable wealth lives right next door to bitter poverty. There's the most beautiful nature and total destruction of the environment. You meet absolutely adorable and open-minded people, but also witness hatred and blatant discrimination. The USA is both very progressive and terribly backward.

These discrepancies drew me to study American Cultural Science at the University of Munich. As a degree, it's not particularly a career booster, but I was keen to learn more about the fabric this nation is made of and how it culturally and politically influenced the rest of the world so massively for decades. Without any doubt, the USA had a tremendous impact on my life ever since I drank my first can of Coca-Cola.

I had participated in races in the United States before, but always in road marathons. Western States would be my first-ever trail race and ultramarathon, and it was going to take place in one of the country's most beautiful places, the Sierra Nevada mountains. For months, I had devoured race reports, YouTube videos, online maps, and photo galleries. And yet, being on site overwhelmed me.

We were staying in Truckee, the next big city to Olympic Valley, about a 15-minute drive apart. Our headquarters was a wonderful cottage in the middle of the woods. It was perfect. Very quiet, surrounded by old pine trees, with direct access to a stunning trailhead close to Donner Lake. The cottage was extremely spacious to grant everyone their private area — a feature that would soon be helpful, if not indispensable.

For the next couple of days, we all enjoyed a much-needed relaxing holiday with great food, good talks, Western States YouTube videos, occasional runs, and familiar hangouts. In short, we had a great time.

As bonus entertainment for everyone who was not running Western States, we found some extra activity. One week before the big race, there was another running event taking place in Olympic Valley, the Broken Arrow Skyrace. The race featured the first climb of the original Western States route. We planned to run it for fun, but half of my crew DNF'ed during a brutal 28 miles (45 km) mountain race that everyone had clearly underestimated. The jet lag and the altitude surely played a role in breaking Michi and Marie during the Broken Arrow Skyrace. But no one was frustrated or upset, and I, personally, took it as another warning that the first part of Western States should not be taken lightly.

More eating and running followed, and before I knew it, race week was just around the corner. The plan for the last six days before the start was to solidify all the strength, all the endurance, all the knowledge and all the ambition for Day X. But things turned out quite differently.

CHAPTER 15
THE PLAGUE, ACT II

" "The darkest hour has only sixty minutes."

— MORRIS MANDEL

R ace week was a complete disaster: a grueling, six-day roller coaster ride that alternated between bad news, even more bad news, and desperate problem-solving.

On Sunday, one week before the race, crew captain Lisa tested positive for COVID-19. It hardly needs mentioning that, as crew captain and wife, she played the most important role in my Western States planning and life in general. The possibility of not seeing her on the course or when I crossed the finish line terrified me. In addition to that, I was also afraid I might catch COVID-19 again, with my long, tough April infection fresh in my mind.

But as everyone knows, when it rains, it pours. One by one and day by day, my whole crew got infected as well. After

Lisa succumbed on Monday, Henning and Christiane tested positive on Wednesday. Michi followed suit on Friday, one day before the race. The last loss in particular was a huge problem. Michi was supposed to pace me. It was a responsible task and essential for the outcome of the race. Besides Lisa, Michi is by far the most pleasant person to run with I know. His presence as a pacer would have been both soothing and diverting. I was convinced that nothing could go wrong if I had him by my side for the last 40 miles of the race. But that was not going to happen.

Marie was the only one who didn't get infected during this demoralizing week. Like me, she had already caught COVID-19 earlier in the year and obviously showed a better immune response than the rest of my crew. Marie was 100% dedicated to supporting and pacing me at Western States, but she had never done either before.

Finally, my best man Chris, who planned to join our party on Thursday, had to cancel his trip to the US because of an overbooked flight. His presence would have definitely given me an extra boost of motivation. I don't know anyone else who loves and hates running at the same time as him. (I was soon caught in this contradiction, myself.)

In the end, we spent the whole week wearing masks, reorganizing our plans, isolating each day's newly infected people, and begging any available deities that Marie and I would stay healthy. In the end, we did. As a bonus, Lisa recovered rapidly and was noninfectious right when the race was about to start. That was what we had to work with.

With Lisa and Marie as my final crew, I didn't have many options for new duty assignments, especially regarding the pacing job. Lisa was back on track, but there was absolutely zero chance she could run the last 40 miles from Foresthill, the point from which pacers are allowed at Western States, to the finish with me. We did everything we could to figure this out, but options were few and far between. I even asked around my fellow runners and their crews if they knew anyone who would spontaneously be available as a pacer, but to no avail. Besides, running side by side for hours with a total stranger would not have felt right. We finally agreed that I would try to run the first half of the night on my own and then be joined by Marie for the tougher, second half. We expected that change to happen at the Rucky Chucky river crossing (mile 78). Lisa, on the contrary, would keep on crewing for the remaining aid stations of the race. But this is not what eventually happened out there. Not even close.

A more than stressful week came to an end with a wobbly race plan and a drastically decimated crew. The Levelhead was in a constant state of shock.

CHAPTER 16
EASING INTO RACE READINESS

> "Anyone can train hard. Do you have the discipline to recover?"
>
> — LAUREN FLESHMAN

Besides all the fuss with my self-dissolving crew, I still had some leftover running to do. I hate tapering intensely because the few remaining workouts before the event are usually neither challenging nor ultra-easy. And often they are shorter, so you have far too much time to sit around and think about things. But every coach I'd worked with so far regarded tapering as a highly critical phase. Karim appeared rather relaxed, though. It might be because a 100-miler is not a road marathon, so there's a little more latitude about peaking. Or maybe it's because he does not believe much actual training or damage can be done during the last week. Either way, here's how Karim designed my very last week of training.

Saturday: 2- to 3-hour long run by feel. I decided to start in Olympic Valley, run up Emigrant Pass, the first climb of the race, do a bit of the High Country that followed and then return on the same route.

Sunday: "1-hour mindful recovery run, connecting with the surroundings, checking external elements and doing a couple of senses scans, checking on how your body feels, along the way." That was Karim's original wording to describe the workout. I started at a trail head in Truckee, just a few meters away from the house we had rented. The trails perfectly mimicked what big parts of Western States would look and feel like. At least I thought so at the time.

Monday: Tempo run. A 20-minute warm-up followed by 10 minutes at a 6/10 effort, 5 minutes easy and another 5 minutes at a 7/10 effort. I did this workout in Olympic Valley around a golf course. Obviously, a very popular route for trail runners doing tempo workouts, since I met quite a lot of them along the way. I felt the altitude, but I was happy that I still managed to push a bit harder.

Tuesday: I asked Karim if I could visit the canyon, and he gave me the green light. I wanted to know beforehand how the heat *really* felt. Henning, Christiane, Marie, and Michi joined me for the self-experiment. The four of us went down to the Rucky Chucky campground and got a good taste of what I could expect on race day. With 106 °F (ca. 41 °C) and ultra-dry, almost static air, we reverently experienced what makes Western States a true behemoth of ultrarunning. We ended our 50-minute jog along dusty fire roads with a much-needed cooling in the actual river I would have to cross on a rope in the middle of the night four days later.

Wednesday: Active recovery run for further acclimatization, followed by 5×20 seconds strides to freshen up the legs. No sooner said than done.

Thursday: Day Off. Boring.

Friday: Easy 25-minute jog by feel, plus a few strides. I guess I was locked and loaded now. At least physically. Mentally, I did not feel tapered one bit.

Despite the difficulties my crew and I had gone through during race week, my tapering left me in some way self-confident and even a bit excited about Western States. I believed that I had done everything I could to prepare myself for this race. I knew it wouldn't be an easy ride, but I was willing to struggle my way through when I would run into trouble. However, I had no idea *how much* trouble I would run into. And how much focus and energy the last six days of stress had taken from me.

CHAPTER 17
BIBS, BONDS, AND THE WESTERN STATES VIBE

> "Western States is not just a race. It is a state of mind, a way of life, a journey of the soul."
>
> — ANN TRASON, *14-TIME WESTERN STATES WINNER*

On Friday, however, all the tension and despair of the past days fell away. Together with my decimated crew, I went to Olympic Valley to pick up my bib number and take part in the race briefing. Western States vibes hit hard, and exactly at the right time. The organizers set up a tiny race expo with a handful of tents and an old-school clipboard type of race registration. I felt distinctively welcomed and appreciated by the volunteers, board members, and fellow runners alike. Everyone was extremely helpful and relaxed. There was plenty of room for worry-free chats and encouraging words. One of the race directors came up to me while I was standing in line, congratulated me for making it here, and urged me to enjoy every minute of the race the next day. The inevitable mispronunciation of my intricate family name also provided some amusement. There were smiling faces all over the place. Yet still, despite all the lightness, everyone knew about the relevance and impact of Western States and was excited about the next day.

I had never experienced such a truly heartfelt and authentic atmosphere at a race before. It was one big family of 384 runners and their crews, race officials, and volunteers. And I was blessed to be a part of that.

The same went for the one-of-a-kind race briefing held after everyone picked up their bib numbers and generous starter bags. Usually, such briefings are compulsory, boring events no one likes to attend. You're being force-fed information that you can look up on the race website (and probably already have) and get an update on the weather, which you also have already checked on your smartphone dozens of times. Well, once more, Western States is thoroughly unique in this regard. The lawn in front of the speaker stand was packed. Runners, as well as their crews and pacers, listened carefully to every single word the race director and board members delivered. There were great speeches, paying tribute to the far-reaching history of the race, as well as to everyone involved. Diana Fitzpatrick, president of the Western States Endurance Run's board of directors, also gave space to the Indigenous groups who inhabited the land the Western States course runs through for thousands of years. This was the first time that these peoples had been acknowledged at Western States and her words were intended to give back to those communities from which the land is borrowed. Renowned painter and race participant Yatika Starr Fields, who is a member of the Cherokee, Creek, and Osage tribes, created a wonderful race poster that says: "Together we will live-breath good." Proceeds from its sales went to the Washoe community and to the Western States Trail Foundation for Environmental Stewardship. It was a moving moment.

Everyone also followed closely the introduction of female and male elite athletes. This illustrious circle included Jim Howard, who won Western States in 1981 and 1983, and was returning to the race after 17 years. And it included Meghan Canfield, participating for the 13th time, having won her age group seven times. All these athletes were celebrated equally, and everyone was amped up about toeing the line side by side the next morning.

This Friday afternoon once again underlined the unprecedented cultural, historical, and athletic meaning of the Western States Endurance Run. It was an honor to witness this first-hand and be a part of it.

CHAPTER 18
LAST WORDS AND FIRST STEPS

 "Showing up at the start line is half the battle."

— UNKNOWN

felt calm in the early morning hours of June 25, 2022. Despite all the strain, I'd slept well during race week. The alarm sounded at 3:00 a.m. and I started my race morning routine: taking a shower, getting dressed for action, pinning my bib number to my shorts, and having a breakfast consisting of two slices of toast with jam, two cups of black coffee, one cup of water, and half a banana. Not particularly a feast, but this menu has proven itself many times.

My crew members, Marie and Lisa, were diligently packing their gear and filling coolers with meals and drinks I had prepared the night before. Everyone was really calm and focused, and we only spoke when it was necessary. Once everything was packed, we got into the car and drove to

Olympic Valley, probably for the 27th time since we arrived in the USA.

It's hard to describe how I felt upon arrival. I wouldn't call it joyful anticipation. But at the same time, I detected absolutely zero tension inside of me. Usually, tension builds gradually during race week and, ideally, peaks at the start line. It helps me stay focused and reminds me that something special is about to happen. I'd been too busy dealing with logistics than to pay attention to my emotional state. But I'd made peace with all the setbacks and was ready to start.

The gun would go off at 5:00 a.m. My shrunken crew and I made it to the start line 15 minutes early, and I got rid of a couple of clothes. We listened to a heartwarming motivational speech by board member John Trent that climaxed with these words: "Three pieces of advice. Run with thanks. Run with love. And run with an open heart. I know we're in a data-driven sport, but that's my algorithm of love and care."

Deeply touched by these words, I shed a secret tear. And before I knew it, Western States was on.

100

Training on my home turf in the **Bavarian Alps**. Just for the sake of Western States, I started practicing with handheld bottles. My plan was to use them to travel light between shorter stretches of the race. *(Chris Drüke)*

Short stony trail section between Pico Ruivo and Pico do Arieiro on **Madeira**. *(Lisa Mehl)*

Jungle-like forest trail close to Curral das Freiras on **Madeira**. *(Lisa Mehl)*

Greek Runcation. On the climb up to **Mount Olympus** on a long training day. *(Chris Zehetleitner)*

Skala *(2866 m)*, the pre-summit of Mount Olympus. *(Chris Zehetleitner)*

Pep talk with my coach, Karim Ramadan, shortly before the start of the Katara Vertical K at **Ursa Trail** in Metsovo, Greece. *(George Savvatoupis)*

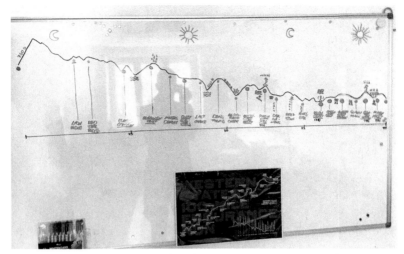

Western States 100 **race script** on the whiteboard in our living room. The sun and the moon indicate day- and nighttime. The little blue waves stand for additional access to water, for example from creeks. The underlined aid stations are the ones with crew access, and the little human icons mark the spots where I thought I would pick up my pacers. *(Chris Zehetleitner)*

4/5 of my crew with their bib numbers for the **Broken Arrow Skyrace** one week before Western States. From left to right: Lisa, Christiane, Michi, and Marie. *(Chris Zehetleitner)*

Tapering run alongside the American River, close to **Rucky Chucky campground**. A foretaste of the grueling Western States heat on race day. Also, the last gear test, such as a bandana on my neck filled with ice. *(Marie Keck)*

Pacer number pickup in Olympic Valley. Although only one **pacer** is allowed to accompany each runner, participants are being handed out 3 pacer numbers and a change of pacer is allowed at any of the last 5 aid stations. At the time we picked up the numbers, only Marie (left) and Lisa (right) were left of my crew. *(Chris Zehetleitner)*

My **race week face** when everything I had planned for months fell apart.
(*Marie Keck*)

Last words of encouragement by longtime race volunteer Jim Richards at the bib number pickup. *(Lisa Mehl)*

Legendary Western States mugshot. *(Western States Endurance Run)*

PART TWO
INTO THE UNKNOWN

CHAPTER 19
STARTING ON FAMILIAR GROUND

T he initial steps of the race felt familiar. I'd run the first 8 miles (ca. 13 km) on a tapering run a few days before. It was also the area where I had watched my crew race at the Broken Arrow Skyrace. It looked and felt different at dawn, though. The air was pleasantly cool, although warmer than you'd expect at 2,000 meters above sea-level, where temperatures can quickly drop below 32 °F (0 °C). A gentle harbinger of the day ahead.

I decided at the last minute to listen to music on the first stretch. I'd brought wireless in-ear headphones for this purpose, and used the music mainly to ground myself, connect with the race, and limit external distraction. Although I love listening to wild, heavy, or fast music, it doesn't work for me when I'm running an ultramarathon. Sure, songs like these deliver an extra boost of energy, but the high art of running long distances is to pace yourself properly and not to explode after two hours of all-out exertion.

To give you a hint of what I was listening to on my climb up to Emigrant Pass, here are a few of the mellow, sometimes even melancholic, songs on my Western States race day playlist:

Bon Iver, "29 # Strafford APTS"
Maylene & The Sons of Disaster, "Drought of '85"
Dan Reeder, "Bitch Nation"
Newton Faulkner, "Teardrop"
Patti Smith Group, "Because the Night"
Snow Patrol, "Set the Fire to the Third Bar"
Tom Rosenthal, "I Go Solo"
Agnes Obel, "Familiar"
Leonard Cohen, "Come Healing"
The Gaslight Anthem, "National Anthem"
All the Luck in the World, "Haven"
Birdy, "Skinny Love"
Novo Amor, "Carry You"
Tuvaband, "Trees"
Bruce Springsteen, "Atlantic City"
Thrice, "Salt and Shadow"

Down, *"Jail"*
King 810, *"Bad Man"*
Trevor Sensor, *"The Reaper Man"*
Bear's Den, *"Sophie"*
Mumford & Sons, *"Little Lion Man (Live)"*
Alt-J, *"U&ME"*
Greg Graffin, *"The Fault Line"*
Tim Barry, *"Prosser's Gabriel"*
The Lumineers, *"Ho Hey"*
NYVES, *"Fools"*

I meticulously followed my race script, or what I could remember of it, and forced myself to completely hike the first 2,500 feet (ca. 762 m) climb on fire roads with only very few strides of running on short flat sections. If there is one basic rule for racing ultra distances, it is to start slow. Painfully slow. You're going to be out there for many hours and you have only one power source. If you exploit it too early in the race, you are doomed. It surprised me that almost everyone around me seemed to be equally smart. A bunch of Levelheads. Those days of killing yourself on the way up to Emigrant Pass, which every race report blog warns against, seemed to be over. Long live the internet and its infinite pool of wisdom.

Emigrant Pass is one of the most legendary climbs in ultrarunning, and I am sorry to demystify it, but: it's a ski slope. The scenery is floodlights, chairlifts, broad paths of compacted soil, with occasional toolbox leftovers such as sledgehammers and wrenches of all sizes by the wayside. Not exactly a romantic image of trail running. Nevertheless, the spirit among our small group of Western States participants was one of a kind. I was running with about two dozen recreational athletes somewhere in the upper midfield. Their faces (and calves) soon became familiar and occasionally took turns in front of me. There wasn't much talking, though. We were all doing our best to stay relaxed and light-hearted. But at the same time, everyone knew that they were starting something big and meaningful.

Then, more quickly than expected, the first climb was over, and we were about to embrace the first of many indescribable highlights of this race: Watson's Monument, which honors one of the trail's originators, Robert Montgomery Watson. It's the highest point of the course with an elevation of 8,750 feet (ca. 2,667 m).

Almost perfectly timed with my summiting of Emigrant Pass, the sun came up. Delighted by this wonderful scenery, I ran through a cluster of spectators who'd gotten up really early and climbed to this epic viewpoint even before the runners. An almost ecstatic, obviously German, spectator identified me as one of the few runners from his home country and prompted me to turn around and behold the sunrise. I followed his advice. Staring at the horizon, I looked at both the short distance I'd already covered, and the long way I still had to go. It was an exceptionally deep moment. I had arrived at Western States.

CHAPTER 20
HIGH COUNTRY AND THIN AIR

Right after sunrise, I entered the High Country, allegedly the most technical part of the race, with rugged singletracks through trees, and dirt trails full of stones, gravel, and tree roots. I don't mean to sound smug, but if you're used to training and racing in the European Alps, it is all very runnable. Because this year's race was predicted to become really hot, I knew I wouldn't have to expect crossing any noteworthy snowfields like runners in other years. Instead, we got wet feet here and there, or tried to avoid it by dancing around small creeks and puddles.

Of all the challenges I'd been expecting on this first part of the course, only the high altitude bothered me. With less oxygen in the air you're breathing, everything feels a bit harder than it should. You can breathe deep, but you feel as if you're not taking enough oxygen in — and the harder you push, the more difficult it gets. I had trained for this and had adapted a bit, after doing most my last tapering runs at high altitude. Still, I monitored my breathing and exertion cautiously, to make sure I didn't go over the edge and waste too much energy. As mentioned before, my plan was to take the first part of the race easy — after all, this was a 100-miler, not a 10k.

And I was surrounded by beauty. California's Sierra Nevada mountains are just overwhelming. It's vast and pristine, almost romantic mountain terrain in a state that hasn't changed one bit for hundreds, if not thousands, of years. The tiny trails we ran on were cautiously carved into nature and meandered around old trees, gigantic boulders, and thick bushes. The racecourse was carefully marked with little flags. And yet small groups of runners got lost in the wilderness every once in a while, albeit only for a few meters. That's how untouched the High Sierras landscape is.

I felt very calm and peaceful during the first part of the Western States Endurance Run. It was a fine start into a long day and even longer night. I settled into a nice flow and ran the longest section between two aid stations, making my way to Lyon Ridge at mile 10.3 without much trouble. I learned to accommodate the altitude and the occasional hiccups caused by the conga line of midpack runners that dynamically contracted and expanded like an accordion. Although my split times might imply otherwise, I can honestly confirm that I ran the first part of my race at an effort no higher than 2 out of 10. Ok, maybe a 3 out of 10. Either way, I did not ignorantly overpace or go out too hard. The Levelhead wouldn't have dared to.

CHAPTER 21
AID STATION ANGELS

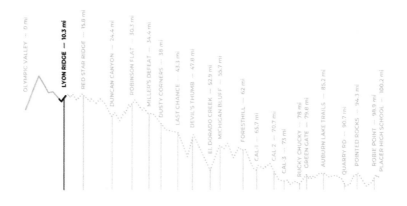

I reached Lyon Ridge (mile 10.3), the first aid station of the race, after a little more than two hours and was in and out of it in under a minute. In ultramarathons, I usually obey the self-imposed rule: "If there's nothing left to do at an aid station, move on."

And all I had to do at this aid station was to fill two bottles of prepared sports drinks with water — a quick and easy task. But it was enough for the volunteers at the aid station to show me how helpful and dedicated they are. They did all the work for me and asked if there was anything else I needed. I gratefully said no, thanked them from the bottom of my heart, and gave them heartfelt props for their great music. I don't remember which song they were blasting, but it was highly motivating for both the runners and the aid station personnel. What a warm hospitality and wonderful atmosphere.

And it wasn't a lucky exception. Every single aid station and checkpoint met this incredibly high standard. All volunteers were 100% focused on the needs of the incoming runners. After a hearty welcome, bottles and flasks were filled with whatever you wanted. Then someone would help you get packed with ice to arm you against the heat. There was no need to explain to them where and how to stow it; they knew exactly what they were doing. Absolute cooling professionals. There was always a well-equipped food table, even at the remotest aid stations. Snacks, fresh fruit, baked goods, warm food, such as soup, and ice-cold soft drinks of any kind. They never seemed to run out of anything. Even as a midpack or back-of-the-pack runner, you were supplied with the same premium offering. Heading out of the aid station, every runner got an extra sponge bath if desired. It was the total package.

This well-oiled aid station machinery is no accident. Volunteers are highly trained, and the assigned captains watch over well-established, bulletproof procedures for each aid station. Everyone takes great pride in their work and the job of supporting runners on their big day very seriously. There is very likely no other race in the world with such great aid station support. And to that, I take my hat off.

Despite the hospitality, I was quickly back on the Western States trail. The psychological trick of mentally dividing a race into smaller parts works really well for me, especially in ultramarathons. That's why I focused solely on the next aid station or checkpoint and not on intervals like one-quarter or one-half of the race. Running 20 times 5 miles is much easier than running 100 miles. Although, as I would learn later, 5 miles can be unbearably far as well. Yet for the first third of my Western States race, time flew by fast and so did the aid stations.

Another useful technique I learned from Karim was to do occasional senses checks. On my way to the next aid station, I checked in with myself by paying attention to what I saw, smelled, tasted, and felt. It takes less than 5 seconds to do, but it can be a mighty tool to refocus and find back into the present moment. My self-check on my way to the next aid station, Red Start Ridge, made me realize I was in a good state, both physically and mentally. I felt blessed and hopeful for a day and a night of running ahead of me, and fully embraced by the race.

CHAPTER 22
WARMING UP ON RED STAR RIDGE

My legs felt great. I was cruising along at an effort that felt highly sustainable, and the Red Star Ridge (mile 15.8) aid station flew past just like the first one had. The following 8 miles (13 km) to the third aid station, Duncan Canyon, however, quickly brought me down to earth. The early morning chill had long gone, and the heat kicked in hard, especially since the section was very exposed due to a wildfire.

I was also realizing that the racecourse mostly goes through completely remote territory. This wasn't clear to me before the event. When you're racing in Europe, you usually pass a few managed huts on every climb and a full-grown village in every valley. Much of the rugged Western States Trail is accessible only by foot, horse, or helicopter, and it can be hours before you see someone who is not a runner or a race volunteer. At this early stage, however, I enjoyed the remoteness and solitude a lot.

I was in the middle of the majestic Granite Chief Wilderness, and reverently followed the narrow paths carved into the rugged backcountry. It felt like the Western States trail had opened its soul to me, with all its depth and beauty. But my ultimate antagonist was beginning to reveal itself, too. The heat had abruptly become a harsh reality of my race. I wasn't yet able to connect the dots, though. During the past months, I'd run hundreds of miles under the unforgiving sun and in her inescapable heat. I had moved my training ground to Mediterranean Greece for a week because it was hot, and did three sweat-inducing races in three days there. I even applied an after-run sauna protocol during the last weeks of my training, to adapt to the heat more efficiently. I thought I had steeled myself for this villain. But I'd gradually learn that this safeguard was wrought by hope, not reality.

I showed up at the start in Olympic Valley in shorts and a t-shirt, which was smart. I saw other runners kicking off the race in full-on cold-weather gear. They were wearing pants, windbreakers, even wool hats. I was relieved that I hadn't fallen into the same trap and was able to ignore the slight morning chills. But along with my summer clothes, I was wearing a race vest that fully covered my back. It was mostly to carry all my sandwiches, gels, and sports drinks. Also, all my clothing and gear was black. Of course — this had been my style and attitude since I was a teenager. But when the heat of Western States turned on, literally speaking, I felt the consequences of my fashion choices.

None of this could dampen my mood. I felt hopeful, curious, and hungry for the miles to come. Even more importantly, I was still relaxed. Memories of my training and my COVID-19 infection popped into my mind every once in a while. I also recalled race week in fast-forward mode, and all the events and experiences that led to this present moment. I was indeed running the Western States Endurance Run. That was all that mattered right now.

CHAPTER 23
THE ART OF POSITIVE SELF-TALK

> "Pay attention to your thoughts, for they will become words. Pay attention to your words, for they will become actions. Pay attention to your actions, for they will become habits. Pay attention to your habits, for they will become your character. Pay attention to your character, for it will become your fate."
>
> — UNKNOWN, ATTRIBUTED I.A. TO LAO TZU AND THE TALMUD

The night before the race, Karim achieved impressive results on the psychological preparation front. We both knew that my mental strength would be a decisive factor in running Western States. We had given this topic a lot of attention during my preparation, already. But now was the time to fine-tune it for the big day.

Usually, we would go through my race script several times, visualizing all the things that I would or could be confronted with. The good, the bad and the ugly. But since the last week before the race had derailed so terribly, he decided instead to work out a very plain but effective positive self-talk strategy with me, instead. In the end, we crafted three core sentences that loyally accompanied me through the first third of the race:

"I am well-prepared."

"I will do my best."

"It's gonna be a different race experience."

When you're out there in the wilderness with pumping lungs, thrashed legs and a hot head, such little sentences can do a lot. So, I brought them to mind as often as possible.

"I am well-prepared" gave me self-confidence and took away some fear, especially of the heat and the sheer distance of Western States.

"I will do my best" took away the pressure to achieve peak performance, but at the same time motivated me to push hard.

"It's gonna be a different race experience" helped me to let go of any previous ideas about how this race should unfold, and all the things that had gone wrong during race week. It also encouraged me to embrace whatever the race could throw at me. After all, different, just like the taste of black coffee, isn't bad. It's just different.

Self-talk is a delicate task. It is frequently misunderstood. Some people believe in the outdated tradition of repeatedly shouting trivial phrases at yourself, affirming how great you are and that you are going to reach your goal. Hoping that loud repetition will make you believe it eventually, and that the body will follow. I am sure you have met these people at races and wondered who the hell they are yelling at.

In reality, self-talk is much more individual than that. Some phrases or words might work for you, but others don't. It totally depends on whether or not they trigger something inside of you. And whether they trigger the desired thoughts and emotions or bad ones. When working on my positive self-talk, I try to pay attention to what a statement or a single word does to me emotively, when I hear it for the first time. If I have to think it through, it's usually not the right one for me. At CCC, for example, the simple word "breathe" did much more to me than the more complicated "It's a great honor to be in this race." I had planned to use both on race day, but soon abandoned the latter, while the former stayed with me all the way from Courmayeur to Chamonix.

The phrases "I am well-prepared," "I will do my best," and "It's gonna be a different race experience" would soon become my last line of defense against an increasingly overpowering nemesis that had just stepped on the Western States stage.

CHAPTER 24
THE HEAT IN DUNCAN CANYON

A t Duncan Canyon (mile 24.4), I kicked off my cooling protocol. I realized I had to stop my body from constantly heating up before it became a race-threatening problem. My dizzy head, especially, was a clear signal that I was on the edge of a heat stroke. The cooling protocol became necessary one aid station earlier than planned, so I was not properly equipped for the procedure. I was wearing a close-fitting black cap that did not accommodate much ice under it to cool my head. I also did not have a suitable scarf or bandana for cooling my neck; the very tight tube scarf I had didn't hold much ice. And finally, I had no arm sleeves with me to fill up with ice. Once again, the volunteers were extremely helpful and attentive. I was already so hot that I couldn't have executed the cooling measures by myself. Simple tasks, like folding my tube scarf into an ice pocket or squeezing ice cubes into my flasks, had become incredibly complicated to me. I didn't panic, but I was surely having serious thoughts about how this would go.

Up to this point, I had been good at drinking my high-carb sports drink and water. I was matching my roughly calculated energy demand and consuming an amount of fluids sufficient to prevent dehydration despite the intense heat. But I realized that I wouldn't be able to swallow any of the real foods I carried with me. These were sandwiches with different spreads that I had tested dozens of times in training and racing. My lack of appetite for any kind of foodstuffs most likely was caused by the heat and its impact on my body. No big deal, I thought.

Oh boy, was I wrong. It was a *huge* deal.

CHAPTER 25
BULL'S-EYE FOODS

> "Give me fu, give me fa, give me tabba sabba sah... Uh!"
>
> — METALLICA, *FUEL*

'll take a little detour here. Let's talk food. Yummy. This is a big topic among runners, but you can actually narrow it down to one simple truth: If you want to race an ultramarathon, you need carbs. A lot of them. But fueling is a delicate task to solve. If your stomach turns its back on you, you are doomed. However, I could proudly say that this had never happened to me before, which I was genuinely thankful for.

While engineered sports drinks and gels can contain a massive amount of carbs and can get you a long way, you will eventually start adding real foods. If you don't, you will most likely get sick of the ultra-sweet packaged stuff and start craving different tastes and textures. Real foods can also play an important role in providing you with salt, which is absolutely crucial at high temperatures. If you sweat a lot, you are not only losing liquid, but also plenty of electrolytes.

Real foods can be anything from sandwiches to pasta with tomato sauce to rice balls or pancakes. If you really want to do your homework well, you test both engineered and real foodstuffs in training and find out which amounts you can consume over what time at what effort. At the end of such an evaluation phase, you will have found your "Bull's-Eye Foods." This term, coined by ultra coach Jason Koop, describes foodstuffs that you can eat any time, in large amounts, even when running long and hard. Bottom line, your Bull's-Eye Foods are what you bring on race day.

For Western States, my goal was to consume about 300 calories per hour. That's about 75g of carbs. That's equal to 1 pancake with chocolate spread, 1 peanut butter and jelly sandwich, 3 potatoes, or 1 small plate of pasta. These examples are not accidental, as they are my actual Bull's-Eye real foods. They are high in carbs and calorie dense, I can eat them any time and love their taste and texture, they include salt, and most of all, I have tested all of them on various training runs and races. My crew can hand these to me at aid stations with crew access, and I can bring most of them on the trail.

My main source of energy, though, was a high-carb sports drink I had also tested extensively. With a whopping 300 calories per 500 milliliters, this drink not only delivers vast amounts of carbs, but also ensures the better part of my liquid intake. During heat battles like Western States, there is a risk of consuming too many carbs, though, if you link them with your liquid intake. However, I had never gotten sick from too many carbs, and I planned to carry one additional flask or bottle of plain water during the day to get some extra liquid without carbohydrates.

The night before the race I stood in the kitchen cooking pasta with tomato sauce, preparing sandwiches, making pancakes, and filling flasks with my sports drink. I also had a small pot cooking for hours on a tiny flame in the back corner of the stove. In it was a simple vegan broth with completely over-cooked noodles. Though this meal was not in any way haute cuisine, it would be my insurance if all other foodstuffs let me down. Or the other way around. I had no idea about the essential role this broth would play later in my Western States roller-coaster race.

CHAPTER 26
ROBINSON FLAT MAYHEM AND CREW LOVE

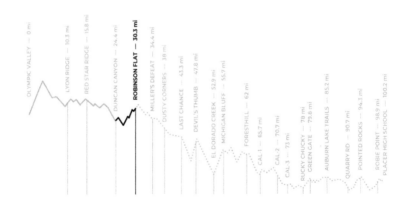

After crossing Duncan Creek, where I took the first of many full-body cool-down baths, a long-ish climb brought me up to Robinson Flat (mile 30.3), the first aid station where I could meet my crew. It was pure mayhem. The place was packed and the noise from supporters, officials, and spectators was earsplitting. If I hadn't been groggy from 30 miles of running and eager to work through a checklist of 27 to-dos with my crew in ideally less than 10 minutes, it would have been a nice party. I know that many people celebrate Robinson Flat for its party vibes, but I found it extremely stressful.

Nonetheless, I was delighted to see Lisa and Marie for the first time since Olympic Valley. It is hard to put into words what meeting my crew during an ultramarathon does to me. On one hand, it feels flattering. Someone is selflessly dedicating their precious time and energy to your running project. They handle lack of sleep, maddening boredom, nerve-wracking time stress, and carry nearly a whole houseful of stuff from one place to another, without knowing if their runner would need any of it. On the other hand, if someone commits to supporting any of my races, they do have a job. I am very straightforward about my needs and sometimes, even before the race starts, I might sound a bit demanding about the dos and don'ts of race day. It's a give and take thing, though, and I have served my fair number of crewing jobs as well.

Henning and Christiane, who had already crewed a runner at Western States three years before, provided a trove of practical knowledge and helpful insider info for Marie and Lisa. Most aid stations, even the ones with crew access, are difficult to reach and involve a lot of driving, bus rides, and hiking. At the same time, you must not be late and miss your runner under any circumstances. Crewing at Western States requires diligent planning and accurate execution, something I did not waste a thought on during my race. I simply relied on meeting my crew at the assigned aid stations.

Lisa and Marie both did a remarkable job in taking care of me and were better prepared than the mechanics at a Formula

One pit stop. I knew I had the best crew in the world and that they would do anything to support me with everything they had. Unfortunately, I had to immediately turn down their very first and most urgent offer: real foods.

The thought of eating any of my prepared foodstuffs literally made me gag. It is a peculiar experience, and every ultrarunner has it eventually. Although your body is in desperate need of carbohydrates, you'd rather let your tank run completely dry than put anything in your mouth, let alone chew and swallow it. Forcing yourself to eat nonetheless is a skill not many ultrarunners master well. In my case, it was completely out of the question to consume any of the meals my crew offered. I once again had to face the truth that training is not racing, and things can derail on race day in ways you never prepared for. On the other hand, what else can you do but repeatedly test things in training and then hope for the best?

What I could consume, though, was coffee. Drinking coffee while racing had worked for me many times, from running up Austria's Stubai glacier at night or turning laps on an acre in Rodgau, Germany, during daytime. Maybe it is because of its special taste. Everything else I usually consume during a race is either salty or sweet. Coffee's bitter taste is a welcome change. I also have an overall positive relation with coffee in general. I simply love all the rituals regarding the preparation and consumption of this magnificent beverage. And the caffeine surely awakes or re-awakes the spirits, which applies to Monday mornings and to ultramarathons. Typically, I force my crew to bring a gas stove and a small moka pot coffee maker on the trail. In fear of igniting a wildfire and also because it is much easier to handle, I switched to a delicious instant coffee I had discovered just weeks before Western States. Finally, a game plan that seemed to work.

Still, I ended up consuming only coffee and water at Robinson Flat — not what we had planned. And also not very beneficial energy-wise for the remaining 70 miles (113 km) of the race.

But what irritated me most was that my legs started cramping heavily the second I sat down in a camping chair. It caught my crew and me completely off-guard. Whenever I moved either leg, a new group of muscles contracted painfully in unnatural ways. After a brief discussion, we identified a lack of salt as the origin of this unexpected problem, one that I hadn't had in any of my previous ultramarathons. The fact that I had not eaten any real foods during the last 7.5 hours had obviously triggered a number of issues besides the obvious carb deficit. I was relying on the salt in my sandwiches and other real foods to cover my needs — but they were still in my race vest. No sodium had entered my body for several hours, but I had sweated out a whole salt mine.

To avoid a chain reaction of subsequent problems, we declared the heat as the root of all evil (instead of our failure to not bring salt tablets) and from now on tried to address it as properly as possible. In the positive column, our well-prepared cooling protocol hit the bull's-eye. The Levelhead sighed with relief. Finally, something that went according to plan. I got rid of my dark-colored, early morning race kit and changed to my self-created, snow-white "Beyond the Heat" clothing line: a bucket hat with small ice pockets and arm sleeves filled with ice. Most importantly, I finally put on my large tube scarf for some extra ice cubes on my neck, the part of the body that radiates the most heat. At least that's what I had read. I also got a new, pre-prepared running vest with cold drinks and everything else I might need. At the last second, Marie handed me a bag of salted pretzels to resolve the sodium issue. Even if I couldn't eat them, I could at least lick off the salt grains. Sounded like a plan. And I was off again.

CHAPTER 27
ONE LAST CHANCE AT MILLER'S DEFEAT

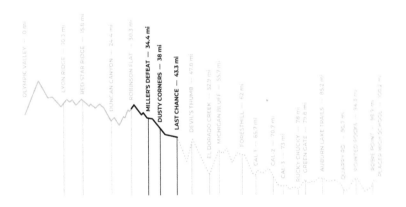

was now about to enter the decisive second section of the Western States 100 course, the canyons. Namely, Dead-wood, El Dorado, and Volcano. Although I'd been on the trail for 50 km already, I still felt okay enough to hike and run my way to the next aid station and mental anchor point. The singletracks and fire road trail climbed the flank of Little Bald Mountain, followed by a long descent to Miller's Defeat (mile

34.4). I didn't feel great, but on the whole, I kept doing what you do in an ultramarathon: I kept on moving forward.

Dusty Corners (mile 38) and Last Chance (mile 43.3) were a different story, though. I was now on the south side of the ridge line I had started running on in the High Country, and the intensity of the heat increased significantly. In a race review, I had read that the views to Screw Auger Canyon on the one side and Deadwood Canyon on the other side are breathtaking, shortly before you arrive at Last Chance. Unfortunately, I don't remember much of this section. I was trying to keep my "s" together, considering the decisive heat battle I was fully engrossed in.

I revived my cooling protocol at each of the three aid stations, Miller's Defeat, Dusty Corners, and Last Chance. They were all well-prepared to satisfy the runners' need to cool down as quickly as possible. I re-filled my arm sleeves, tube scarf, and bucket hat with ice and got an occasional ice water sponge on my neck, all with the indispensable help of volunteers who knew exactly what to do. I also started putting ice cubes in the back pocket of my running vest to get a bit of extra cooling on my back. But I completely forgot that my sports drink powder was in that pocket. It ended up being one sticky, slimy, and heavy mess on my back. I would soon be unable to consume my sports drink anyway, so maybe it wasn't a great loss.

These cooling measures were my last hope. They worked differently on different parts of my body, though. Effectiveness ranged from awesome to nothing. While the ice cubes on my neck seemed to deliver a constant and pleasant chill for about 1 to 2 hours, the ice in my arm sleeves would disappear within minutes after I left an aid station. The arm sleeves themselves almost disappeared, as I had lost a significant amount of weight already. Mostly water, of course. My arms were now much thinner than during my last-minute shopping frenzy in Olympic Valley the day before, where I bought those snow-white arm sleeves. They were too wide now and constantly slid off my arms. Even more tricky was the cooling of my head. While pouring ice water over it at an aid station worked just fine, putting ice cubes under my bucket hat was a different story. It created brain freeze after a few minutes. I felt like I'd eaten ice cream too quickly. I was constantly reorganizing the ice under my hat to avoid this unpleasant sensation.

In sum, my cooling methods all felt great for a short period of time. Overall, however, they seemed to be a drop in the ocean. It was a hard truth for the Levelhead, but his control over the Western States race was quickly slipping away.

CHAPTER 28
NEGOTIATING WITH THE DEADWOOD HEAT

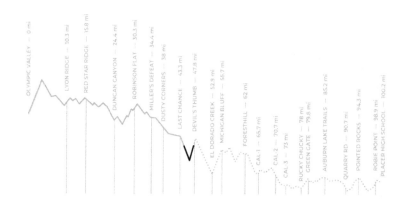

 "The heat doesn't care how tough you are."

— JASON KOOP

Up next, I began running through Deadwood Canyon, one of the three hottest points of the race. Its topography, with the sun reflecting from the steep hillsides, and almost no air movement, makes this place incredibly hot. The heat was insane. I desperately changed my effort level, trying to find a sweet spot: I didn't want to produce too much heat from pushing too hard, but I also had to keep moving forward. My singular aim was to reach the next aid station, so I could do another cooling procedure. I negotiated with the heat fervently, but I couldn't prevail. It simply would not let me gain ground without drowning in dizziness and fatigue. Yes, drowning. That's how it felt.

I had experienced the notorious Western States temperatures a couple of days before, when I'd decided to go on a tapering run in the Canyons. I caught a good day and got a more than convincing demonstration of the shimmering heat. During my short 50-minute jog along dusty fire roads, I tried to build a relationship with my antagonist. Or at least find an agreement for race day. I would respect her by not pushing too hard, and in return, she would let me pass until sunset. I was confident that this agreement would work out on race day, but it didn't. Just like the mountain sometimes does not let you pass, the heat would not allow me to run in those canyons as I wished.

Meanwhile, I had slowed down significantly. The heat in Deadwood Canyon felt thick and viscous, making every step, movement, and even clear, thinking three times as hard as normal. I felt like I was inhaling burning air that heated my body with every breath I took. With a blurred vision and an obscured mind, I realized that I was not the one in control anymore. It clearly was the heat.

To make things worse, I had completely given up on my high-carb sports drink. My body just would not let me sip on that flask. Even thinking about it almost made me throw up. The only thing I could take was plain water. I had used this sports drink in races and long workouts for months and years. It never let me down. Until today. My body was completely out of order. Nothing seemed to function properly. Even worse, instead of working on possible solutions for this looming disaster, I seemed to care less and less about my demise. The Levelhead and all his game plans was at his wits' end. I was doomed.

After a steep descent into Deadwood Canyon and passing a swinging bridge, I submerged myself head to toe in a small pool from a spring coming off the canyon wall. The cramping in my legs when I went down was almost more than I could handle, but it was worth it. It provided a true glimmer of hope. I was not the only one who regarded this cooling spot as a last life safer — I was pressured out of my bathtub after a minute by two other overheated runners waiting impatiently. Despite the phenomenal heat and the harm it had caused to my system, just one quick plunge into cold water restored me to an almost acceptable level. Sadly, not for long.

Even though my situation had worsened dramatically, the thought that my race was becoming a giant failure didn't cross my mind. My brain was unable to see the bigger picture anymore. I was in sheer survival mode.

CHAPTER 29
A DEVIL'S THUMB

The climb following my dip in the spring went up to the notorious Devil's Thumb (mile 47.8), named after its iconic rock formation. This was my undoing. I knew it would be difficult: a sheer 2,000-foot (ca. 610 m) ascent with 36 narrow switchbacks carved into the canyon wall. I vaguely remembered my race script for this section, which sounded a little like this: "It's the hardest climb of the race. There's nothing you can do about it. Just get it done."

That's what I did. But the only thing that was done was me. Halfway through, I wasn't hiking or running, I was zombie-walking up the steep canyon path, brain-dead, staggering, and utterly depleted. With every step, I felt my last reserves of energy slipping away. Making progress had become an agonizingly slow and arduous ordeal. My legs felt like anchors, resisting any attempt to lift them from the scorching ground. I must have looked like a struggling survivor of a natural disaster as I inched my way up this seemingly never-ending climb. My dizziness and fatigue had become truly enervating. I had a front-row seat to watching myself slowly pass out.

I have absolutely no idea how I made it to the Devil's Thumb aid station in the end. I cannot recall anything from the second half of the climb. Zero memory. But somehow, despite my devastating physical condition, I reached the top. The next thing I remember was a compassionate volunteer asking me what I needed. I dizzily slurred: "Nothing. Just a break."

A few seconds later, I had collapsed on a camp bed, my whole body shivering and cramping. It must have looked like a scene from *The Exorcist*. I had lost all control over my limbs and torso. I was trembling and twitching like a fish onshore. Strange noises resounded through my chattering teeth. I folded my arms tightly around my chest to slow down my spasms. It didn't work.

At this point, I realized the harsh truth. This race was over for me.

Although quitting a race is a painful and terrible decision to make, it gave me an immediate mental boost. It was a relief. After all, abandoning can feel like liberation from the distress you're in. Once I knew I didn't have to run another 50 miles (80 km), a great tension inside of me eased. In fact, my Level-head saw his opportunity to play it safe and get out of this alive. Sure, a part of me was sad that it would end this way. But it was alarming to see how quickly and willingly I succumbed to the decision to drop out of Western States, the race I had dreamed of for so many months.

But what exactly had happened? Even from the perspective of months post-race, I find it difficult to say just how I got into such a bad condition. It must have been a mix of hyponatremia, which is basically a lack of salt, along with heat stroke and extreme fatigue. My inability to eat for half a day surely didn't help much. Whatever the symptoms or pathology of my state were, the root of it all was the heat, a reason as banal as it was frustrating. After all those months of preparation, including extensive heat training, I still fell victim to the most obvious challenge Western States has. What can you do?

I was brought back to the here and now of Devil's Thumb by a bestial swarm of mosquitos and an elderly woman offering me some vegan broth. I'd been laying on the camp bed for a few minutes. Or was it many minutes? I honestly don't remember. What I do remember is her words: "You need to get out of this aid station and get moving!"

It was not the message I wanted. I was expecting — even hoping — to be taken to a medical tent, where someone would cut off my participant wristband, give me an infusion and put me on a shuttle back to Auburn.

Well, there is no medical tent at Devil's Thumb. Neither is there a shuttle. Like many other aid stations of the Western States Endurance Run, Devil's Thumb sits in the midst of the Sierra Nevada wilderness. I only had one option. As the woman said, I had to get moving. So I did. Someone at the last camping table of the aid station handed me a Waldmeister popsicle as a farewell gift, and I was out of Devil's Thumb, back on the trail and off the beaten track. I was devastated.

This was the lowest physical point of my race. Of any race, I had ever done. Of my entire life, for that matter. But I was about to enter an even darker place, a place situated deep in my mind and anchored in the darkest days of my life story.

CHAPTER 30
THE INMOST ELDORADO CANYON CAVE

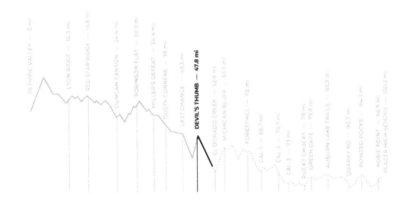

fter I left Devil's Thumb aid station, I was still in terrible shape and absolutely convinced that this race was over for me. At the same time, the realization that I could neither walk back nor muster the energy to continue terrified me. But things were about to get worse. Much worse. I had 8 miles to go (13 km) to Michigan Bluff, the closest point that my crew could put me in a car and end my misery, and I spent it entrenching myself in the most self-loathing, self-humiliating, and demeaning thoughts since my mid-twenties. Undoubtedly, the worst time of my life. I had, mentally, arrived in hell.

My upbringing was somewhat troublesome. When I finally broke free to start my own life at the age of 19, I carried a large bag of bad interpersonal experiences, but had no tools to handle them. An unhealthy, non-stop, on-the-road musician's lifestyle did the rest. I was continuously running myself down without realizing it. It was a time of tormenting self-doubt, not knowing where I belonged or where I wanted to go, and uncontrolled auto-aggression. Mentally and physically. Even though I later worked on this difficult stage of my life with the help of a therapist, it still took me years to build the self-confidence that, for example, allows me to write these lines today. Heck, it's still not easy.

I have come a long way during the past 20 years. I usually regard the occasional emergence of such old feelings as dusty remnants from the past. Distant memories will shoot into my head, but then disappear as quickly as they came. These flashbacks happen extremely rarely. But on the trail to Michigan Bluff, they literally *exploded* in my head. I heard negatives voices telling me I'm a failure:

> "What a fucking idiot you are to believe you could run Western States. You don't belong here — this is a race for real ultrarunners, not wannabes like you."

> "You are such a disappointment to everyone who believed you could do this."

"All the work and support your friends and crew put into this project, it's all in vain, and it's your fault."

"You really flew around the globe for this? Pathetic."

"There's nothing you are good at. You are just pretending all the time."

"Everyone else already knew you would fail. They just didn't tell you. You were the only one who thought you could do this. How naive."

"You have zero grit. When the chips are down, you always fail. That's just who you are."

Over more than three hours, I ran myself down until nothing was left: no love, no respect, no self-worth, and no care for myself. It was completely devastating.

I'd lived a drug- and alcohol-free life since I was 16, so I was used to being confronted with dark thoughts and disturbing feelings, simply because I refused to consume any substances to repress them. I regarded this as a good thing, though. It trained me to regularly reflect on what's going on inside of me and find ways to deal with it. But what I faced between Devil's Thumb and Michigan Bluff was neither revealing nor an opportunity to grow. It was outright spiritual self-destruction.

It was not only my heart and my soul that shattered: my brain went berserk on me, too. It was utterly degrading to catch myself mentally writing an Instagram post about my DNF. In fact, I wrote a series of three posts about it, and I had every single word written in my brain. It was a nice mix of good and cheap excuses, rendered in a very convincing, believable tone. When I realized what I was doing, I was deeply embarrassed and got the feeling that I wasn't only deceiving myself, but also everyone who followed my Western States journey. It felt terrible.

CHAPTER 31
NOTHING LEFT BUT COUNTING STEPS

've been through low points in other ultra races before. I knew they belong to the sport. But I also knew they'd eventually disappear and allow me to continue, as if nothing had happened. This time it was different. The profoundness of my discomfort and deteriorated mental and emotional state were unlike anything I had ever experienced before in either running or life. I remember saying to myself: "This is not how I want to race."

That's a testimony I would reconfirm any time. But such declarations don't help you much when you are in the midst of a 100-miler in California's most remote backcountry. In fact, such thoughts only make things worse.

Speaking of making things worse, I had just entered the next canyon: El Dorado. On this endless 2,600 feet (ca. 792 m) descent, further exposed to direct sunlight, I was again stumbling more than running or hiking. I don't remember much of this part of the race, although I do remember my race script, which says: "This is the hottest point of the race. Get out of there as quickly as possible!"

I had now reached a section of the Western States Trail that has a strong historical connection to the Gold Rush era. Remnants of old mining operations and bygone artifacts from pioneers once seeking a fortune kept on popping up in the vast landscape. I wasn't chasing gold or adventure. I just wanted to escape the terrible predicament I was trapped in. But that redemption seemed to be completely out of my reach.

Around El Dorado Creek (mile 52.9), a little more than halfway through the race, I was so burnt out that I had to count steps to keep on moving forward. It's a mental trick that I usually use for the last 2 kilometers of a fast half-marathon or 10k. It has just the right amount of brainwork to distract me from fatigue and pain, but it's also simple enough for the brain to execute. I counted every second step from 1 to 100 in English while visualizing the numbers in my head. Then I started from over. I have no idea how many rounds I did, but there were a lot, until I finally reached Michigan Bluff. The aid station where I could meet my crew, finally drop out of the race, and end my misery.

CHAPTER 32
TOUGH LOVE AT MICHIGAN BLUFF

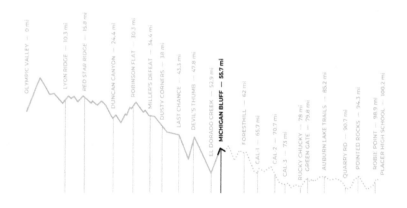

S hortly after 8:00 p.m., one of the worst days of my life was almost over. I was entering the old mining town of Michigan Bluff (mile 55.7) after one last long, gradual climb. A great sense of relief overcame me. I had finally made it to the place where my suffering would end. I immediately searched for the aid station captain to get rid of my racer's bracelet, the symbolic act that would turn my DNF into reality. Unfortunately — or fortunately — Lisa found me before this could happen. She convinced me to spend a moment with my crew and escorted me to the little home base she and Marie had set up at the back of the aid station hours ago. Once they talked me out of giving up immediately, they calmly gained an overview of my situation. Due to bad network connection, we hadn't been in touch since Robinson Flat, 25 miles (40 km) and eight hours ago. They had absolutely no clue what I had been through since then.

I sat down on a camping chair, the legendary piece of mobile furniture that has countless DNFs on its conscience. The community of ultrarunners lovingly calls it "The Chäir." Myth succinctly explained: "If you get comfortable, you're doomed."

In my case, there was not much left to doom, so I had no scruples about taking a seat and soliloquizing about what had happened. Meanwhile, Lisa and Marie encouraged me to change my dirty, stale clothes and try a few real foods. They were carefully arranged all around me, but I hated all of them. The foods, not Marie and Lisa, of course. But there was one thing that didn't make me want to choke. It was the ridiculed rescue meal, overcooked broth with soggy noodles. I thought ironically about the real foods I'd prepared the night before, only to find myself eating the simplest of all. But it was a true lifesaver. Even its minimal amount of carbs could resurrect my body, and the salt would stop my cramping seizures. Note to self: always bring soup to your ultra races. And never make fun of it again.

After the soup, I maneuvered myself into an argument with Lisa and Marie about the end of my race. I had believed that they would acknowledge my critical state, immediately accept my decision to drop out, and take me back to Truckee in our crew vehicle. I was very wrong about that.

They calmly listened to my complaints and horror stories, but at the same time insidiously preparing me to continue the race.

> "Oh yes, I see you're still shivering. How about changing your shirt?"

> "Yeah, the cramping is bad. I bet that hurts. Wanna try a spoon of soup?"

> "What do you want me to fill up your bottles with?"

> "Look, here's your head lamp. The batteries are full. I checked them."

> "More soup?"

I felt like I was being both infantilized and manipulated. Like a child being talked into a visit to the dentist. Against her will, but also for her own good. And it was about to get even more underhanded.

Lisa and Marie updated me on the race situation. Of course, they knew about my ABC-Goal. Before the start, we agreed that they would not give me any info on timing, except when I got within 1 hour of the cutoff, which was my situation when I entered Michigan Bluff. To be more precise, I was about 30 minutes behind the predicted 30-hour pace and 1 hour before the cutoff time of Michigan Bluff. That's the point when officials would close the aid station and take everyone out of the race who was still sitting in "The Chäir." I didn't understand why Lisa and Marie suggested I should still tackle the next section of the race, a rather easy 6.3-mile (10 km) stretch to Foresthill School. As I saw it, this simply didn't make any sense.

After a wholly ridiculous and pointless 35-minute discussion about cutoff times, average paces, physical damage, fatigue, and carbohydrate deficit, I found myself stepping out of the aid station with two hand bottles and Lisa as a pacer by my side. I had no idea how exactly that had happened, but the proposal to just hike to Foresthill for fun, and thereby surpass the longest racing distance of my life, didn't seem too daunting. And Marie would be waiting there with the crew vehicle.

The only thing I could say was, "Whatever, fine with me."

And we were out.

The **High Country** is, without any doubt, one of the most beautiful places on earth. *(Chris Zehetleitner)*

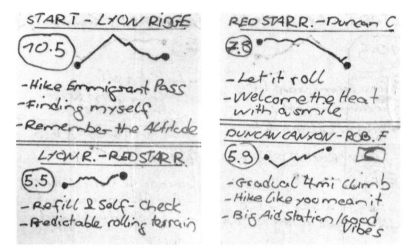

START - LYON RIDGE

(10.5)

-Hike Emmigrant Pass
-Finding myself
-Remember the Altitude

LYON R. - RED STAR R.

(5.5)

-Refill & Self- check
-Predictable rolling terrain

RED STAR R. - Duncan C

(7.8)

-Let it roll
-Welcome the Heat
  with a smile

DUNCAN CANYON - ROB. F

(5.9)

-Gradual 4mi climb
-Hike like you mean it
-Big Aid Station/good
                  Vibes

I carried some **Notes to Self** with me during the race. I didn't look at them during the race, but I knew their content by heart. These little notes were the essence of my Western State race script. The "C" stands for "Meeting my **Crew**" *(Chris Zehetleitner)*

Running into the intense Western States heat at **Cougar Rock** between Lyon Ridge and Red Star Ridge aid stations. My watch is turned inward. I would rather not spend any thought on tracking, time, distance, or pace. *(Facchino Photography)*

Cooling down at **Duncan Canyon Creek** between the aid stations
Duncan Canyon and Robinson Flat. I started to realize that I'm in trouble.
(Facchino Photography)

Meeting my crew at **Robinson Flat**. Finally, getting rid of my black clothes and picking up my heat-kit. *(Marie Keck)*

Arriving at **Michigan Bluff,** determined to get my yellow Western States wristband cut through and quit the race. *(Lisa Mehl)*

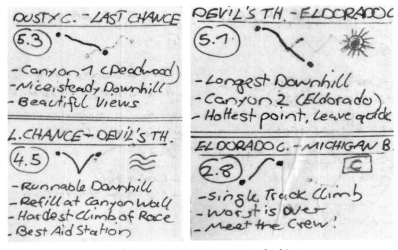

DUSTY C. - LAST CHANCE
(5.3)
- Canyon 1 (Deadwood)
- Nice, steady Downhill
- Beautiful Views

L. CHANCE - DEVIL'S TH.
(4.5)
- Runnable Downhill
- Refill at Canyon Wall
- Hardest Climb of Race
- Best Aid Station

DEVIL'S TH. - ELDORADO C.
(5.7)
- Longest Downhill
- Canyon 2 (Eldorado)
- Hottest point, Leave quick

ELDORADO C. - MICHIGAN B.
(2.8)
- single Track Climb
- worst is over
- Meet the Crew!

More **Race script notes** that I carried in my pocket. It's highly ironic, what my race script said about Devil's Thumb: "Best aid station". *(Chris Zehetleitner)*

Lisa accompanying me to my crew space at **Michigan Bluff**. My Western States race on a razor's edge. *(Marie Keck)*

Because the night belongs to… runners. Hiking from **Michigan Bluff** to
Foresthill with my newly added pacer, Lisa, but with only one head
lamp. *(Lisa Mehl)*

CHAPTER 33
JOB FOR A PACER

> "The whole idea of a pacer is that your brain can shut off a little bit."

— SCOTT JUREK, *EAT & RUN*

Adding a pacer to your race can change a lot, especially when you're running 100 miles. It really makes a difference to have someone by your side to talk about and solve minor and major issues, or simply chat with. Actually, the following aid station, Foresthill, is the earliest point where runners are allowed to pick up a pacer at Western States. There's an exception to the rule, however. If you arrive at Michigan Bluff after 8 p.m., you can be joined by your pacer there. I guess this is because of the impending darkness. It is much easier to run with two headlamps instead of just one. I don't remember the exact time I left Michigan Bluff, but Lisa and I were a team of two now — albeit with only one head lamp. Marie and Lisa hadn't expected me to arrive that late at Michigan Bluff and left their headlamps in the car, a 10-minute bus ride away from the aid station. But we managed to move forward with one light. I'd done it for hours the year before at CCC, when I guided a desperate runner with a broken headlamp from Tete Aux Vents peak all the way down to Chamonix. Remembering that incident as I slowly moved through the darkness of the Michigan Bluff historic mining district, I felt my first positive emotions in hours and let myself recall what had happened at CCC.

When I arrived at the top of CCC's last and exceptionally steep climb, the Tete Aux Vents, I was completely cocooned by thick fog. I made my way through this rather technical section of the course, a barren landscape of massive rocks and seemingly no marked path. After a while, I heard someone calling for help. I spotted a runner whose headlamp was either broken or out of battery power. She could neither move forward nor back because it was pitch-dark all around. Without much thought and very few words, I offered her my help.

We ran very close together, so she could utilize my "truck light" as well. The trick is not to stare at the back of the runner in front of you, but always over their shoulder or on the trail whenever it makes a turn. Switching to the mandatory backup lamp at the next aid station of La Flégère didn't improve her situation. The joke of a headlamp she pulled out of her crammed running backpack was no match for the dark woods we were about to enter. So, we calmly continued our tandem journey all the way down to Chamonix, where we split up about 2 kilometers before the finish line. Amicably, but with very few words.

Lisa and I did the same between Michigan Bluff and Foresthill. It was a simple and playful task that I could handle well. It also made time fly by.

CHAPTER 34
VOLCANO CANYON ZOMBIE WALK

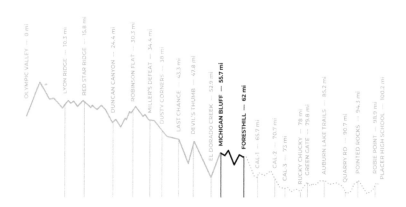

We had entered the Volcano Canyon, the third canyon of the Western States race. It starts with a dirt road out of Michigan Bluff, progresses as unthreatening, runnable singletracks through the canyon, and ends with a long climb on pavement up Bath Road. At the bottom of Bath Road there was supposed to be an additional aid station manned by the Auburn Running Company. Either we missed it, or we simply arrived there too late. It was almost 10 p.m., and I was among the last few runners on that part of the course, one of a zombie army of leftover participants and their pacers that no one would have betted on to finish. That was the vibe I felt.

On my way to Foresthill, I was still convinced that my crew would finally let me drop out of the race there. So, I just enjoyed the hike, feeling a little melancholy, and calmly chatted with Lisa about running and life. It gave me a pervasive feeling of comfort to have her by my side. Lisa is absolutely remarkable in letting me be myself, regardless of what mental or emotional state I'm in. On our two-hour hike, she managed to create a truly caring and loving atmosphere and set my tortured soul more and more at ease.

Once in a while we were passed by another runner-pacer duo. I didn't really pay attention, though. They were in their world, and I was in mine. Theirs included hope, ambition, and grit. Mine was soaked with surrender, disenchantment and, yes, relief.

What I did not consciously realize while walking up Bath Road, though, was that I was feeling better with every step. I even ran a few strides here and there. With the setting of the sun, it was also much cooler. Whatever had happened in Michigan Bluff, it restored my ability to continue the race. But I just didn't get it. Yet.

CHAPTER 35
LEAVE ME AT FORESTHILL

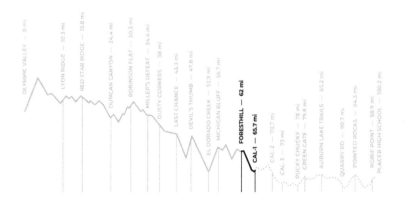

F oresthill (mile 62) is one of the busiest aid stations of the Western States Endurance Run. That's mostly because it's easy to access by car and somewhat late in the race, when most runners are in desperate need of support. Unlike Robinson Flat, Michigan Bluff, or Rucky Chucky, for example, crews don't have to take the bus to reach their final destination. Thus, Foresthill is basically always lively, blocked by one camper after the next. Most crews take the access as an opportunity to offer their runners full-service support, including all sorts of medical, culinary, and psychological assistance.

I recognized Foresthill from the Western States footage I'd seen on YouTube. The elite runners were on fire when they ran down the little dirt path on the side of the long straight road, leading into town. My time of being "on fire" during Western States, literally speaking, was luckily over. The temperature had graciously dropped to a mild 77 °F (25 °C) and the unforgiving sun that had grilled me all day long was gone for good.

At Foresthill I was once again sitting on a cooler, my substitute for "The Chäir," arguing like a mad man that it was finally time to face reality and put that DNF stamp on Western States. The Levelhead came back from the dead and brought forward two brand-new and, at least in my opinion, very conclusive arguments. First, we had fallen even further behind that 30-hour pace that I would need to finish the race. And second, there was the risk of me collapsing somewhere between Foresthill and Rucky Chucky, a section of the race with no crew or rescue access. That doesn't convince you? No? Neither did it convince Lisa and Marie.

At this point, my obsession with dropping out of the Western States had become a weird form of art, somewhere between self-sabotage and cowardly shirking. At the same time, I can honestly say that I was 100% sure that my overall condition and the life energy I had left would not allow me to go on for 38 more miles. To me, collapsing on the trail somewhere between the next two aid stations, Cal-1 and Cal-2, was preordained. And even if I had managed to continue hiking my way to Auburn, I would surely not make it before the assigned cutoff times at each aid station, let alone the strict 30-hour barrier of the finish line. I was totally convinced that this was my Western States reality.

Lisa and Marie took notice of my refreshed DNF campaign, but stoically repeated their treacherous protocol from the last aid station and prepped me for yet another stretch of the race without my explicit agreement. Their premier weapon of choice was once again the overcooked noodle soup, the one that had brought life back to my defunct organism at Michigan Bluff. Plus a revitalizing cup of coffee. Or two.

The next section of the racecourse would be a steep downhill to Cal-1 (mile 65.7). Before I could even realize what was going on, I was out on the trail again, and Lisa was back by my side as a pacer. Now we had two headlamps instead of one. Things were getting better and better. But I was still caught in my negative thought spiral of a prematurely terminated Western States.

Safety-conscious Levelhead made a deal with Lisa and Marie. I would run down to Cal-1 "just for fun" and then hike all the way up again to, you got it, finally drop out of the race once I was back at Foresthill. I even instructed Marie to wait for me there, instead of driving to Rucky Chucky, which would have been the next aid station with crew access. Later, I would find out that this was a stupid request with far-reaching consequences. Luckily, one runner and his pacer came toward us shortly after we had left Foresthill. This reassured me that my plan to run down and up the canyon and then call it a day was absolutely legit.

Cal-1 was only 3.5 miles (5.6 km) away, on playful singletrack down into the American River Canyon. The heat of the day had now given way to complete darkness, so my greatest threat was gone. A distant memory of my debit and credit list came to mind. It said that I could handle running at night very well. In fact, I even liked it. Without admitting it to Lisa, or to myself, for that matter, I almost enjoyed the run to the bottom of the canyon. Almost.

It took us about one hour to get to Cal-1. The aid station was ultra-small. Not much to see or do there, but guess what? I took another seat in "The Chäir" and started promoting my inevitable DNF one last time. Only minutes later, my Western States race would be turned inside out and upside down by an old lady.

CHAPTER 36
AN OLD LADY AND THE ULTIMATE BOON

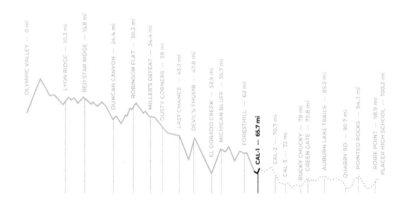

started getting angry. I was tired of having to explain my precarious situation over and over again. Likewise, I hated not being taken seriously, something that seldom happens in real life. My arguments about cutoff times and traveling speed were weighty, and my condition was still critical, I believed. What didn't Lisa understand? Why wouldn't she let me end my race?

Because I was wrong. So wrong, and somehow Lisa knew it. I was fit enough to resume running, and all I'd done at Michigan Bluff, Foresthill, and now Cal-1 was waste precious minutes, if not hours, with futile discussions. Yet, I insisted on proper counterarguments to prove me wrong. The Levelhead inside of me had taken full control of my thinking and acting. The Punk had been tied up and gagged. It was a deadlock situation.

There were a handful of exhausted but engaged runners refreshing themselves at Cal-1. Every once in a while, new ones came in. I took note of this coming and going and heard myself saying: "None of them is gonna make it to the finish on time. I wonder why they even try."

I don't remember if I said these words out aloud, mumbled them to myself, or just voiced them in my head. In any case, they were a pathetic projection of myself onto the world around me. If I had given up all hope, then I had to think there was no hope for anyone else, either. I was locked up in my self-created prison cell.

Meanwhile, Lisa was desperately trying to call or text Marie to discuss the possibilities of a pickup at one of the two upcoming aid stations. She was clearly running out of ideas about how to trick me into running "just one more stretch." Endorsing a potential pickup at Cal-2 seemed to be the only option she had left. But without confirmation from Marie, she couldn't offer it to me. But there is absolutely zero mobile network on Cal Street. Lisa tried over and over again with both of our phones. Two networks, zero signal. I watched the spectacle from my chair and wallowed further in self-abandonment.

Until an old lady volunteering at Cal-1 finally resurrected me. She had been busy handing out cans of cola and words of encouragement to other runners. Then she spotted me. She walked up to my seat of sorrow, bent down to look me deep in the eyes, and spoke the following words: "You get out of this chair. Now. This is Western States!"

100

PART THREE
RESURRECTION

CHAPTER 37
MIRACLE ON CAL STREET

> "You get out of this chair. Now. This is Western States!"
>
> — OLD LADY AT CAL-1

er words hit me like an atom bomb. It was a moment of merciless enlightenment. My Western States epiphany. A rush of anger and shame flowed through every cell of my body. I felt exposed. My cover was blown. The old lady, a complete stranger, was right. So goddamn right. I wouldn't have dared to veto. But even more, I finally remembered why I was here. It *was* Western States. You have no place here if you don't either give it all and ultimately collapse or make it to the track at Placer High School. There are no other options. I realized Western States wouldn't let me go until I could no longer move, or I crossed the finish line.

That was the very last push I needed. Fired up by this over-whelming emotional release, I left everything behind, including my pacer and my phone, and went on a 30-mile sprint to the finish line. In one second, I literally burst into a sprint. It was redemption time. Everything that had seemed so complicated and bleak had abruptly disappeared, and only one thing mattered now: running like hell.

What followed was the most intense racing, if not running, experience of my life. It felt like this was the reason I was put on earth. Shorts, a shirt, running shoes, a headlamp, and two hand bottles of water were all I had and all I needed. The agony, the dizziness, and the fatigue were entirely gone, and I started flying up and down the trail with just one simple desire burning inside of me: to run.

After my physical and then mental collapse near Devil's Thumb, the Ego had taken over completely:

My body is destroyed.
My will is broken.
My race is over.

Final and ultimate truths that were irreversible, or so I believed. But when I leaped off my chair and stepped on to the trail, I entered divine ground. I had shifted from the Ego to the Self. The old lady was the personification of my Self, giving my Ego a gigantic kick in the butt.

Although I am 78% sure that the old lady was real — a part of me still believes that she was just a delusion — she was the messenger of something that I had been carrying inside of me. Something that we all carry inside of us since birth, and even before that and beyond death. The Self. However, I never experienced it as clearly and as transformatively as in this moment at Cal-1.

The Punk inside of me had been unleashed. Head over heels, reckless and full of life. My mental prison was completely shattered, and I was running with my heart. Rational thoughts gave place to raw emotions and a completely unleashed life force. Never had I undergone such a radical transition so rapidly and thoroughly. It was like a switch had been flipped, taking me from self-abandonment and hopelessness to total liberation and unbounded relief. I felt pure freedom, an all-encompassing state of flow. It was nothing short of a life-changing experience. It was magical.

CHAPTER 38
FIFTEEN ROLLERS, ONE ELEVATOR SHAFT, AND A SIX-MINUTE HILL

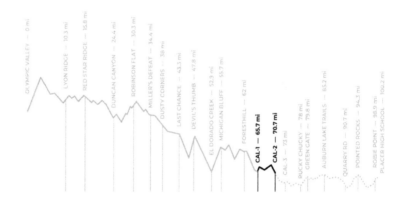

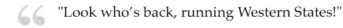

> "Look who's back, running Western States!"

I later learned that Cal-1, the site of my Western States epiphany, is the exact same place on the course that the elite athletes usually start racing seriously. Most likely, they skip the part where they waste hours philosophizing about their forthcoming DNF. But still, Cal Street, also known as the Cal Loop, is a highly decisive section of this race, which makes it even more thrilling that I caught fire exactly there.

Halfway to Cal-2 (mile 70.7) I switched my Garmin display to "average pace," an emergency mode I had prepared in case I got close to the cutoff time. I was well off the pace I needed for a 30-hour finish, so I started working off the deficit second by second. Since I was now running 5- to 7-minute kilometer (ca. 8- to 11-minute mile) splits for the next 13 miles (21 km), it didn't take long until I was approaching the magic average pace that would give me a 30-hour finish. I was flying by dozens of bewildered runners who obviously had a more consistent pacing strategy for their race than I had.

On my way to Cal-2 I passed The Rollers, a section of 15 short climbs, and The Elevator Shaft, a steep downhill on rugged terrain — or that's how they were described in various race reports. But I found it all very runnable and gained ground rapidly. I was obviously benefitting from Karim's countless Rolling Hills workouts. In fact, I didn't even realize if I was going uphill or downhill. I kept a surprisingly steady pace and let it roll.

I gulped down half a can of cola at Cal-2 and refilled my hand bottles with ice water. It took me less than a minute, and I was in my element again, plowing through nocturnal miles, nothing holding me back. Not even Six Minute Hill, a surprisingly steep climb on a fire road. Yes, the Western States race-course flattens out toward the end. But with a total elevation gain of 18,090 feet (5500 m), it still had a number of surprises left, even after I'd already tackled the big climbs in the first half.

The trail gently followed the American River's winding course. Although I couldn't see the river, I clearly felt that I was close to water. Every so often I recognized the silhouette of rocky outcroppings, weathered giant stones that seem to guard this beautifully rugged part of the Western States trail. I enjoyed the solitude while I moved along effortlessly.

For a brief moment, I wondered what Lisa did after I bolted out of Cal-1. But I wasn't concerned. My heart was beating only for the task at hand: running like there was no tomorrow. I also knew that I could rely on her. She would handle things. No matter the cost. And as I'd find out later, the cost for her was high.

CHAPTER 39
DOUBLING UP ON COLA

E ntering the absolutely remote Cal-3 aid station (mile 73), I realized that I would definitely not sustain my revived effort if I didn't get some carbs. Frantically gulping down half a can of cola every 1.5 hours just wasn't enough to fuel the hungry engine that brought me back into the race. Since I was still choking on real foods, I asked the volunteers to fill one of my handheld drinking bottles with cola instead of water. Instead of calculating calories, I settled into a pragmatic "better than nothing" attitude regarding fueling. It worked. I was full of energy and moving fast. But I don't think it was carbs alone that kept me going.

I know this sounds like a movie, but even hours after my Western States reawakening, I still felt completely liberated from all the anguish and distress that had piled up during the day. Like an entirely different person. My sole purpose was to run this race. With all my heart and everything that I had left inside of me — which was a lot more than I would have believed at the Cal-1 aid station.

It was much more emotional than physical. Sure, the cramps, shivering, and pronounced fatigue had disappeared. But the true miracle was my transition from total hopelessness to unbounded enthusiasm and unbreakable zest for action. I thought of the old lady at Cal-1 and smiled.

I was now en route to the legendary Rucky Chucky aid station, where I would cross the American River on a rope in chest-deep water. I'd seen countless pictures of this small-scale expedition and had dreamed of doing it myself for a long time. It was about to happen, but first I had to run another long, almost flat stretch through the night. The race-course unfolded on broad fire roads, narrowed down to singletracks through waist-high meadows, and then back to rocky pathways alongside the river, audible in the darkness.

Eventually, I passed the section I had test-run before the race. I didn't recognize much, though. Last time I was here, I was weighted down by the stifling heat and blazing sunlight. Now, I was lightheartedly cruising through the muggy darkness of the night. Intimidating awe had given way to placid anticipation.

The Western States racecourse becomes much easier in the second half, and even easier in the last third. Whatever time you might have lost in the High Country, the canyons or sitting in "The Chäir," you now have a chance to regain it all. If you are still able to run, that is. If not, this section becomes a nerve-wracking, never-ending hike that will bring you close to the 30-hour cutoff mark or beyond. None of this bothered me. I was too busy doing what I had come to do.

CHAPTER 40
THE PARALLEL CREW UNIVERSE

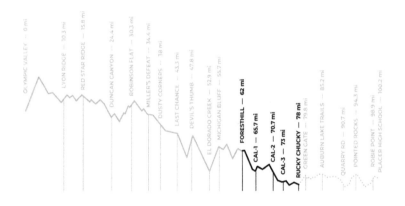

eanwhile, Lisa and Marie were having their own, separate Western States race. After I left Lisa at Cal-1, I had no idea what either of them were doing. I secretly hoped Lisa had followed me and asked a couple of fellow runners and aid station personnel to send a message to my abandoned pacer. I wanted Lisa to know that I was doing fine and that I would love to meet my crew at Rucky Chucky (mile 78). This plan didn't work.

Playing Telephone, however, worked surprisingly well. Lisa later told me that she got all my messages. Unfortunately, with absolutely zero signal or internet connection on Cal Street, she couldn't reach Marie to update her on what had happened since we left Foresthill. While I was trying to run the most negative split Western States had ever seen, Marie was still in Foresthill, back at mile 62, waiting for me. She later reported that she was the very last human in what had become a ghost town after the last runners passed the aid station. Marie eventually received outdated text messages from Lisa asking her to come to Cal-1. Or Cal-2. Or Cal-3. Although the Foresthill aid station personnel assured her that there was no way to reach any of those aid stations by car, she nevertheless decided to give it a shot. Marie drove alongside Cal Street with the racecourse on her GPX watch, but she couldn't find access to pick up Lisa, or me, or both. She didn't know where we were, anyway. Well, the aid station volunteers were right: Cal-1, Cal-2 and Cal-3 were out of reach for her. As a result, Marie cluelessly drove on to the next aid station with official crew access, which was Rucky Chucky, hoping to meet any of us there. What else could she have done?

At the same time, Lisa, still with no signal, had no other option than to run all the way to Rucky Chucky as well. What was planned to be an easy, post-corona-conforming 3-mile hike turned into an energy-sapping 22-mile (35 km) long-run adventure through the night. With two smartphones in her hand, one of them useless because of a locked screen, Lisa was desperately trying to reach Marie while running. The request for a pickup at Cal-1, Cal-2, or Cal-3 obviously were obsolete. The new plan would have been to meet at Rucky Chucky. Ideally, all three of us. But that never happened.

I later asked Lisa what was going through her head while running along Cal Street. She told me she had three concerns. First, she was worried that she'd find me lying collapsed somewhere on, or off, the trail. Second, that I was disqualified by race officials because I had abandoned my pacer. (This was an obviously unjustified assumption based on something she had read in the Western States race rules some time ago.) And third, that I was running so well and fast, that I would arrive at Rucky Chucky before Marie or her would be there to crew me. And this is precisely what happened.

Lisa and Marie both made it to Rucky Chucky and happily reunited there. Unfortunately, I had already passed the aid station and the river, so they packed their crewing gear, brushed their teeth, and headed out to Pointed Rocks, which was the next opportunity to meet me.

In retrospect, it feels like I had handed the baton of mental stress to Lisa and Marie. While they were desperately trying to find solutions for insoluble problems, I was running free, my head muted and my heart on fire. All that mattered to me was to run. Which I did fervently.

CHAPTER 41
WITCHING HOUR AT RUCKY CHUCKY

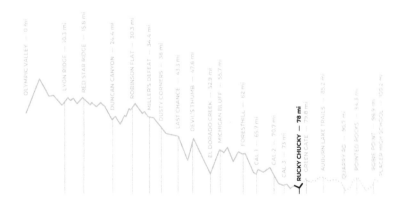

The Rucky Chucky river crossing is one of the most crucial parts of Western States. It's a true highlight for every participant regardless of when they reach it, whether in the afternoon or in the middle of the night. I arrived at the lovely on-site aid station at around 2 o'clock in the morning and was welcomed by several applauding volunteers who told me I was the only person to come through still running. I was flattered to hear that, and I was, in fact, still feeling great — as if Devil's Thumb had never happened. When talking to Jose Rodarte, the Rucky Chucky aid station captain, I informed him that I had lost my pacer and asked him to tell her I was doing fine and that I was happy. He would later supplement my message for Lisa with the following words: "The runner that passed here was a different one than the one you saw at Cal-1."

Hearing this was the greatest relief for Lisa. She later shared with me that this was her magic moment at Western States. Just as the old lady who scared me out of my DNF-chair was mine. It's those sentences you never ever forget and that give you goose bumps even years after they were spoken: priceless memories for a lifetime.

I also asked Jose Rodarte where the runners' crews had set up and scanned the allocated area. I still hoped, at least a little, that Marie had made it to Rucky Chucky on time and I could have some more of that lifesaving noodle soup, a sip of coffee, and a pair of fresh socks for after the river crossing. But there was no crew waiting for me. Well then, never mind. I remembered a particularly smart part of my race script that provided an excellent piece of wisdom for this exact incident: "No crew, no problem. You can do it on your own."

This game plan is a wonderful example of Levelhead and the Punk collaborating. I shrugged off this setback, filled up my hand bottle with cola, and confidently continued where I had left off.

The actual river crossing is a fantastic micro-adventure inside the big adventure of Western States. How racers get to the other side depends on the water level: they're either put in a dinghy or allowed to wade across, clinging to a rope. This year we were doing the crossing by foot. Light chains led the way down to the river, where a whole army of dedicated volunteers helped each runner step on the right stones through the hip-deep water. The volunteers stood in the cold river all day and literally knew every potential tripping hazard in front of them. I later called them "stone agents" because they led the runners through the river so profession-ally, it almost appeared to be a military operation. And for good reason: after 78 miles (ca. 125.5 km) of running, it can be quite a challenge to negotiate a shaky rope, river rapids, slip-pery rocks, and wobbly legs.

On the other side of the river, as a last adventure-playground challenge, we runners climbed a sand hill on another rope before heading to the next aid station: Green Gate (mile 79.8).

Despite losing some hard-earned minutes during the river crossing, I found this episode of the race extra joyful and refreshing. My feet were soaked and freezing, but my heart was full, and I slowed down a bit for the first time since Cal-1 and used the gradual 2-mile climb to assess my situation. I knew I was still moving significantly faster than the average pace that would allow me a 30-hour finish. And I was doing well. Sure, "doing well" at mile 78 of an ultramarathon means my whole body hurt like hell. But none of the aches and pains were bad enough to deter me from continuing the race. I knew it was still a long way to the finish, but I wasn't scared or discouraged. Not even a tiny bit.

It was 3 a.m. Ultrarunners very often report having hallucina-tions and out-of-body experiences when running at night, particularly during the so-called witching hours, between 2 and 4 a.m. These are the hours during which the runners' circadian rhythms tell them in no uncertain terms that they should actually be asleep. Luckily, I was spared from such experiences at Western States. The closest thing to delusions I had to face was at Cal-1, when I was absolutely convinced that I was being attacked by thousands of ants. My micro-panic-attack was quickly shut down by Lisa, who convinced me that I was not in immediate danger. She did confirm that there was indeed one tiny ant scuttling up my neck. I was glad she said that. It proved that I had not gone insane — yet.

The short climb up to Green Gate was very calm and peaceful. There was no one else around, so I was free to enjoy the meditative squishing sounds of my soaking-wet socks and shoes. A true "here and now" moment.

CHAPTER 42
FORGIVING MYSELF AND OTHERS

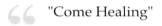 "Come Healing"

— LEONARD COHEN

O ut of nowhere, a song popped into my head. It was "Come Healing" by Leonard Cohen. I had listened to it earlier in the High Country, but since I had left my phone with Lisa at Cal-1, I hadn't listened to music for many hours. The imaginary song sounded so real, though. It was like Leonard Cohen was walking next to me, whispering the lyrics right into my ears. I realized that I had never really paid attention to the words of "Come Healing," despite the song's absolute beauty. Yet, the fragments I could clearly hear and understand made me cry.

I am not a religious person, but I understand this song's theme of mercy and forgiveness. It's about forgiving others — but also about forgiving yourself. When I "heard" it at Western States, I immediately embraced this concept. "Come

Healing" made me realize that I had forgiven the Western States' heat for crushing me. Likewise, I had forgiven me for abandoning myself. I felt peace.

"Come Healing" also made me think about my dad and my brother. For some reason, I link both of them to Leonard Cohen. I believe they both had a phase in their lives when they listened to his music a lot. Maybe they both still do. It reminded me that there had always been family issues, even many years after my parents got divorced. I pondered what the concept of forgiveness could have done for my brother, my dad, my mom, and for myself. It made me wistful, but also grateful. As I write these words, I wonder how they'll feel if they ever read this.

CHAPTER 43
A GREEN GATE AND 20 MILES TO TRIUMPH

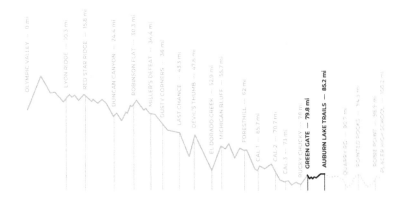

At the tiny Green Gate aid station (mile 79.8), its captain, Grant Carboni, gave me an unrequested update about where I stood in the race. Although I knew I was on the sunny side of the 30-hour mark, his words rung like gospel in my ears: "You've got 7 hours left to run 20 miles. You could even hike it through."

This extra boost of motivation gave me instant goose bumps. Reaching the finish in under 30 hours wasn't just likely at this point: it was almost guaranteed. At least that's what it felt like. I continued my journey with even more confidence and composure. But before I left, I asked Mr. Carboni how far it was to the next checkpoint. The reply came quickly: "Just 5 more miles."

That's the same straightforward answer I'd get at basically every aid station from now on.

I left Green Gate behind and promptly found myself on beautifully rolling terrain, at least as far as my headlamp showed. Otherwise, I was immersed in all-devouring darkness. I could handle both the darkness and the late hour. My vision was clear, and I was wide awake. In contrast to the antagonistic heat, the darkness was supportive. I felt safe and in control. The night put me into a quasi-meditative state and I never even tripped or stumbled. It was like being on autopilot, or as if I was the blindfolded Luke Skywalker, using the force to fight with my lightsaber against that combat remote after Obi-Wan Kenobi told me to use my feelings instead of vision.

Ok, ok. Running through the night was also fairly easy because of the superb headlamp I'd brought. It was a truck-headlight level of brightness. It lasted on maximum power for most of the night, with only one battery swap. Fortunately, I found a spare battery pack in the back pocket of my shorts. Marie had put it there at Michigan Bluff. It was a smart thing for her to do. Changing batteries in the pitch-black darkness of the remote wilderness was not easy, and without my phone flashlight, I had no secondary light source to help. It was a one-shot scenario. I put the head lamp on the ground, held both connection cables tightly, and unplugged the old battery.

I was immediately in total darkness. Blindly fumbling with the cable of the new battery pack, I said to myself, "Let there be light" and there was light. It's such side quests within the big challenge that makes trail running such an exciting sport.

Auburn Lake Trails (A.L.T.) was up next. It was a larger aid station with great medical support. I remembered how I'd been kicked out of Devil's Thumb despite my critical condition. Although not as critical as I'd thought at that moment. I remember saying to myself at Devil's Thumb: "This is not how I want to race."

In retrospect, moving on was the right decision, even though I wasn't the one who made it. When Marie and Lisa went over my head and decided for me, I found it rude, even reckless. But the volunteers and aid station captains, not just at Devil's Thumb, knew very well what they were doing. Many years of experience have taught them to distinguish between a runner who may as well continue the race after he or she is done pitying him- or herself, and a runner for whom the race is definitely over. I am glad I belonged to the first group, although it took me until Cal-1 to finally realize this. From there on, I was not only able to run, but longing to do it. And that didn't change until I reached Auburn.

The only thing that slowly started to become a bit of a problem were my feet. The river crossing had soaked my socks and shoes with water and filled them with dirt. With every step, my soles rubbed on the shoe, and gradually large blisters grew on both feet. According to the plan, I'd be handed a pair of fresh, dry socks at Rucky Chucky that I could put on at the other side of the river, but as you know, I missed my crew. Ironically, I *did* have a pair of spare socks with me. Marie had put them in the front pocket of my hand bottle at Michigan Bluff, and I was carrying them with me the whole time. But through the race, they'd been soaked with water, cola, and sweat and were completely useless at this point. Eventually, I figured that my feet would hold out until I crossed the finish line, and everything after that was completely irrelevant for me right now. Spoken like a true ultrarunner, who cares not about his feet!

But I was right about my feet. I was also right about the rest of my body. It would carry me all the way to Auburn with no permanent damage. The feeling of discomfort during an ultramarathon can be a tricky one. Issues that might be considered sickness or injury in normal life can often be considered minor aches during an ultra. On the other hand, though, continually feeling extreme discomfort can play tricks on your mind. You might lose the connection to your body and miss the point when you actually start feeling better, or when you completely destroy yourself. In my case, the former led to a wholly premature decision to end the race. Thankfully, no one took me seriously.

CHAPTER 44
THE DAWN OF THE AUBURN LAKE TRAILS

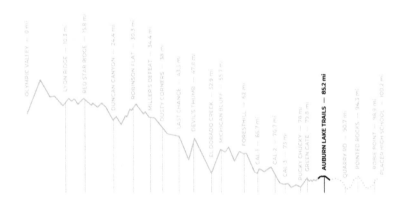

W hen I reached Auburn Lake Trails (mile 85.2) I was almost exactly 24 hours into the race. My thoughts wandered toward the runners who had set themselves a certain time or placement goal for Western States. If you run the course in under 24 hours, you receive a silver buckle; the sub-30 finishers receive a bronze one. Despite having the greatest respect for everyone who can handle that extra pressure, I still believed that my ABC-Goal decision was the right one for me for this race. After all, it was my first 100-miler and I literally had no idea what I was doing. My learning curve was extremely steep, though. I assume that my next race of this distance will turn out a bit less dramatic. On the other hand, the number of things that can go wrong in an ultramarathon is endless, and you are never safe, no matter how experienced you are.

A short chat with my assigned aid station volunteer ended with my obligatory question of how far it was to the next aid station: "Just 5 more miles."

What a surprise.

Shortly after leaving the aid station, the day's first light allowed me to switch off my headlamp and enjoy the sunrise somewhere in the middle of the Auburn Lake Trails. The temperature rose immediately, but with only 15 miles (24 km) to go, I knew that the heat would not become an overpowering antagonist again.

I had run through a whole night with very limited visual input and equally rare social interaction. I was emotionally and literally very much by myself, and it felt great. There'd been a few moments during the night, however, where I felt a bit jealous of everyone around me being accompanied by their pacers. They were chatting, laughing, mourning, and exchanging words of sympathy while throwing up on the trail. The Western States website has its own pacer portal, where more or less experienced runners can offer their duties to participants who didn't bring a pacer to the race. If the decline of my original five-person crew had not happened at the last minute, this might have been an option for me. On the other hand, running side by side with someone you barely know during the tougher part of a race, when nerves are often on the edge, can easily backfire. Just imagine a pacer who is talking your ear off. Or if he or she doesn't run your pace but goes just slightly faster. Or falls behind because of a lack of fitness. Or gasses nonstop about his or her own glory days, like winning an age group at the legendary 1996 half-marathon in Wilsonville, Oregon. I'd rather run alone. After all, doing so allowed me to dive deeply into the present moment many times. There's a lot to be found. It's not only about blurring out the past or future. It's about gently becoming aware of what's going on inside of you with every step and every breath, then letting it go, no matter if it's good or bad or in between. During a few quiet moments on those Auburn Lake Trails, time didn't matter. Neither did distance nor movement. Everything just happened. For a reason.

CHAPTER 45
THANK YOU, SCOTT

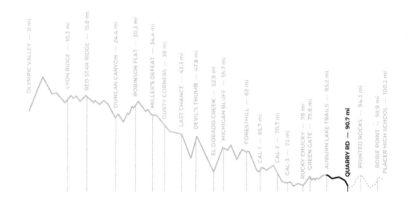

After a very runnable section of the racecourse with a couple of nice creek crossings, the next checkpoint was Quarry Road (mile 90.7). I could hear this aid station from almost 2 miles (3.2 km) away. When I entered it, I found out why. Volunteers had pointed the speakers of their very potent sound system directly into the woods. I don't remember which song was playing, but it surely was some '80s or '90s rock classic, volume cranked to 10. I followed my usual sophisticated nutrition plan and filled one hand bottle with ice water and one with cola.

As I added a handful of chips to the menu because I was still a bit worried about my salt intake, I saw a tall guy standing right next to me, giving runners tips for the next stretch. A chip fell out of my mouth as I realized it was my only running hero, Scott Jurek. I babbled something clever like: "Oh, hey, nice to meet you!"

At least, I hope something that coherent came out of my mouth. Scott asked me if I had lost my pacer. I confirmed this and attentively listened to his helpful hint to watch out carefully for a sudden left turn a couple of miles into the next stretch. He also told me the following: "Just 5 more miles to the next aid station."

Well, thank you, Scott.

I am no one's fanboy, but I can frankly say that no other runner or running book author has had a bigger influence on me than Scott Jurek. Indeed, it was his book *Eat & Run* that introduced me to ultrarunning and the Western States Endurance Run. I wish I would have told him that at Quarry Road. Nevertheless, the extra motivational boost hit hard, and I delightedly continued my race, still driven by a vibrant heart and a muted mind.

After running along the American River on a broad fire road and then back to a singletrack climb, the route's next stop was Pointed Rocks (mile 94.3). It was the second-to-last aid station, and a special one. After exploding out of Cal-1 and running with hardly anything but my heart for 25 miles (40 km), I would finally meet my crew again. And I was really looking forward to that.

CHAPTER 46
POINTED ROCKS REUNION

My obligatory "5 miles to next the next aid station" took me up a short climb, and then over the legendary Highway 49 crossing. It was a former aid station and the place where Jim Walmsley took a wrong turn in 2016. He ended up in 20th place despite having run a groundbreaking race up to that point. By the time you reach this highway, you haven't seen proper roads or any other signs of civilization for hours. It felt unreal when a police officer suggested I might speed up a bit to cross the road between two cars he had stopped for me. Officers, cars, roads, traffic signs... I realized I was very close to finishing the race and fulfilling my dearly desired ABC-Goal.

Running the last meters into Pointed Rocks on a dusty single-track over a vast meadow was like being in a movie. Blades of dry grass gently leaned in the warm summer wind. Finish-line vibes were all around as the aid stations showed up behind a small hill. My crew was there, and I smiled at them to show that I was alright. In fact, I was not only alright, but truly serene. I wasn't feeling extroverted joy or sparkling happiness, but a calm and quiet feeling of deep contentment. Lisa and Marie were well-prepared and offered me all kinds of stuff, from headphones to real foods to cooling measures. I had already become so used to running with nothing but my heart that I only asked for the usual water and cola. Plus a pacer. Finally, a pacer.

Contrary to the original plan, I had been running Western States basically all by myself. Technically, I had Lisa running a few miles behind me all the way from Cal-1 to Rucky Chucky, but that was not exactly how the pacer's job is supposed to be done. Of course, it wasn't Lisa's fault that I rushed off like a 100-meter sprinter after that old lady had given me a piece of her mind. And it wasn't my fault that Lisa, barely recovered from her COVID-19 infection, had to run all the way to Rucky Chucky. What happened at Cal-1 was liberating and, without any doubt, determined the course of my race. Sure, it came at a cost. But it was also the magic turning point when I stopped mentally seeking the DNF and started listening to what my heart actually longed for: becoming a Western States finisher.

It took Marie just 30 seconds to pin on a yellow pacer bib number, and we were out, leaving Pointed Rocks and beginning the last 5.7 miles (9 km) of the Western States Endurance Run. I said to myself: "Just 5 more miles."

It was a felicitous change to finally have someone behind me to chat with. The first question I asked Marie was who had won the women's race. I was thrilled that Ruth Croft made the cut, but it made me even happier that Luzia Buehler from Switzerland had finished fourth, which was just outstanding. She's a great athlete and a wonderful person, and if I hadn't been running myself, I would have followed her race on my screen at home.

Marie and I were running and chatting along, as if we were on a casual Sunday stroll through the Olympic Park in Munich. I am not saying this to boast about my resilient body or tough mindset. In fact, my body was battered and my mind rather clouded than focused. But I was running with my heart, a state you find only when you let go. And that's what I did when I jumped out of that chair at Cal-1 and finally resumed what I had come for.

But before the much-longed-for finish in Auburn, there was one last, iconic, stop to be made.

CHAPTER 47
ARRIVING AT A BRIDGE WITH NO HANDS

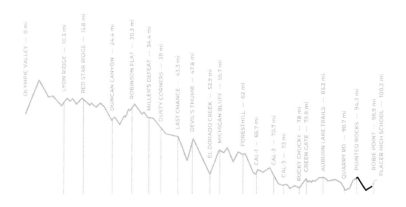

Marie and I cruised down a stretch of gently sloping singletracks that took a sharp right turn and revealed something truly magnificent: No Hands Bridge. I'd been staring at it for seven months, having made it my computer's desktop background photo right after I won the Western States lottery. It prompted a lot of daydreaming and became a place I longed to see. And now, here I was, about to cross it.

The Mountain Quarries Railroad Bridge, as it is officially named, spans the north fork of the American River and was built in 1912. It got its name from a daredevil Tevis Cup rider, who crossed the bridge — at that time guardrail-free — after dropping his reins and saying: "Look! No hands."

For most Western States runners, No Hands Bridge is where they realize they will undoubtedly make it to the finish in Auburn. With only 3.3 miles (5.3 km) to go and 96.8 miles (156 km) in their pocket, it feels like a final spurt. If you have been running all day, and in the case of most Western States participants, also all night, this landmark brings incredible relief.

When I entered the bridge, I stopped running and walked over it slowly. It's hard for me to describe the feelings I had at that moment. The word that best encapsulates them is *arriving*. Not at a certain place, but inside myself. Despite all the lightness and ease I felt after I exploded out of Cal-1, I still experienced an extra amount of redemption while walking over No Hands Bridge. It was an intense moment that still gives me goose bumps as I write these lines.

Arriving is something that I am constantly longing for as a runner. Literally, as in crossing the finish line, sure, but even more so figuratively. I still haven't been able to fully understand why it was that running became my second true love after music. Maybe because it grants me a feeling of accomplishment, of doing something on my own and all by myself. Running gives me a clear goal to work toward and a good chance of reaching it. Or failing and trying again. But eventually, I know I will always arrive where I want to be.

To me, it was nothing short of a miracle that I had come this far. Even when I was not busy trying to convince everyone of my planned DNF, I still secretly doubted I would make it to No Hands Bridge at all. But I had arrived. And now there was only one climb and a handful of miles left between me and my Western States finish.

CHAPTER 48
COMING FULL CIRCLE

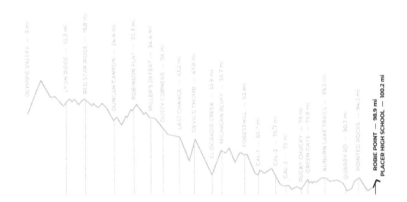

Over broad fire roads alongside the north fork of the American River, Marie and I fought our way up one last grinding climb. Our destination was Robie Point (mile 98.9), where we would meet Lisa again. From Robie Point, all crew members and any friends are allowed to run the last mile with their runner, all the way to the finish at

Placer High School. On the way, we passed the legendary Mile 99 Party, with an enormous amount of applause and shouting for every runner who makes it this far. After a short downhill into town, we crossed the White Bridge.

And just a few meters before the gate to the legendary Placer High School track, I discovered the crew I'd left in sickbay: they didn't want to miss out on the glorious moment which was about to happen. Standing on the sidewalk at a virus-safe distance from other runners and spectators, they looked as if they had just survived a pretty tough night, too. Trotting by Michi, Christiane, and Henning, side by side with Marie and Lisa, I realized once again that my Western States finish was a team accomplishment. Without their selfless support, I would not have made it this far.

I passed the gate and entered the track. I could instantly smell the tartan under my feet, which had been heated by the sun already. Lisa and Marie left these last meters to me and took a left turn to wait for me at the finish. Here I was, running on lane 3 of the infamous Placer High School track with tears of joy in my eyes and deepest gratitude in my heart. This precious moment felt like an eternity: an unfiltered, disembodied, and deeply engraving eternity.

Despite hundreds of on- and offline spectators, running on this track was a very calm and private moment for me. I was all by myself and with myself. My body, mind, and soul were in complete harmony. I don't think I ever felt so complete and serene in my life. Nothing mattered. Everything made sense.

I stepped over the timing mat and simply stood there for a couple of seconds. Then I leant forward and touched the ground with my right hand to reconnect with the lively world around me. My senses sharpened and a burst of happiness rushed through my system like a cold shower. I got up again to receive a medal and a hug from a smiling finish line volunteer, stepped over to the barrier where Lisa was waiting for me and dived into her loving arms. I had finished the Western States 100.

CHAPTER 49
HAVING ARRIVED

L*ife-changing* is a big word. I don't use it often. In fact, I don't think I've ever used it to describe anything I've experienced. But this race has surfaced things that I have never touched before. Both good and bad. It has reconnected me with the pain and the power inside me. In doing so, it has transformed my awareness of what I am able to endure and what I'm capable of accomplishing in life.

I doubt that I will do many other races in my life that grant me such intense encounters with myself or such profound inspiration. The Western States Endurance Run truly justifies its undisputed reputation as the most iconic ultramarathon in the world. And the sensation of running 100 miles for the first time will, of course, happen only once in my lifetime. I'm convinced that the combination of both intensified the overall impact of this event on my life many times over.

As I write these words, many weeks have passed since that day: the calm early morning hours in the High Country, the unexpectedly early introduction to the heat at Duncan

Canyon, the disruptive climb up to Devil's Thumb, the complete physical and emotional void at Michigan Bluff, the mind-blowing resurrection at Cal-1, the excitement of the Rucky Chucky river crossing, the sense of having arrived when strolling over No Hands Bridge, and the infinite inner peace I felt when I entered the track in Auburn. All the memories give me goose bumps and emotionally drag me right back into the race every time they come up.

Having arrived. This No Hands Bridge feeling is also a great way to describe my whole Western States experience. I talked to my best man, Chris, the other day. He knows how much I hate talking on the phone, so he kept it short: "Western States has changed you. You are much calmer now. It seems you have arrived where you want to be as a runner. As a human. That's the vibe you spread. And it fits you very well."

Western States has taught me, among numerous other things, that the true feeling of accomplishment lies beyond the metrics of distance and time. To be deeply and lastingly satisfied with *what* you've achieved and *how* you got there, you have to also find out *why* you were doing it. My Western States journey has closely reconnected me with why I run. With why I pursue anything in my life at all. And therefore, I am blessed.

100

Fairy lights (and sharks) lead the way to the legendary **Rucky Chucky** river crossing, where volunteers are waiting to help the runners make their way through the waist-deep water. *(Lisa Mehl)*

The actual **Rucky Chucky** river crossing. With a low water level and only light currents, runners were allowed to cross the river by foot. And yes, I'm having the time of my life. *(Facchino Photography)*

Running out of **Pointed Rocks** after picking up Marie as my pacer. (*Marie Keck*)

Strolling over **No Hands Bridge**. A profoundly deep and moving moment. *(Marie Keck)*

On my way to Auburn alongside the **American River**. *(Marie Keck)*

Last refreshment at **Robie Point**, one mile before the finish. *(Marie Keck)*

Reunited and closely entwined with Lisa and approaching the legendary **Mile 99 party**. *(Marie Keck)*

Running into **Auburn** with my crew, Marie (left) and Lisa (right). *(Henning Lenertz)*

Approaching **the gate** to the Placer High School track. *(Henning Lenertz)*

Final lap on the **Placer High School track**. Despite thousands of on- and offline spectators, an exceptionally private moment. *(Facchino Photography)*

Finish line vibes. *(Henning Lenertz)*

The Finish. Standing still for a few seconds. Shortly after, I wiped the sweat off my face and touched the ground with my right hand to reconnect with reality. *(Marie Keck)*

PART FOUR
THE AFTERMATH

CHAPTER 50
THE GOLDEN HOUR OF A GOLDEN RACE

You learn a lot about racing if you look at it from the outside. All the excitement, all the thrills, the struggle, the pain and relief, the doubt and the fulfillment. We humans usually try to avoid such intense physical and emotional experiences in life, especially if there's a risk of failure and disappointment involved. Yet still, some of us dare to show up at the starting line, tackling yet another running goal that seemed to be impossible a couple of months or years ago. Racing is pure bravery, if you ask me. It reveals giant parts of our true nature and calls forth mental, emotional, and physical strength that remains mostly hidden in our daily lives.

The golden hour at Western States describes the last 60 minutes before the strict cutoff time of 30 hours. Every year, almost a third of finishers cross the line within this motivating time frame. It is a great tradition to cheer and celebrate the golden hour runners just as much as the top athletes, who arrived almost 15 hours earlier.

Although lottery luck plays an important role in getting into Western States, I believe not one single runner who throws their hat into the ring does not dream about finishing the race. Despite its highly competitive nature and its elite status even among the top athletes, it is still the greatest honor and biggest accomplishment to complete the Western States Endurance Run within the 30-hour cutoff time. It's an epic goal that 70-year-old runner Gunhild Swanson achieved in 2015 with a time of 29 hours, 59 minutes, and 54 seconds. She was the first woman in her age group to ever finish the race and was accompanied in her last mile by Rob Krar, the male winner of that year. It is stories like this one that make the golden hour at Western States one of the most thrilling and heartwarming sensations of our sport.

My crew and I remained at the high school track in Auburn until the last official finisher crossed the line after 29:55:48 hours. It was very moving.

CHAPTER 51
BUCKLE UP

About an hour after the official cutoff time of 30 hours, the awards ceremony took place. It was a warm-hearted and touching event that gave space to every single finisher, from the winners of the race to the golden hour runners. One by one, every finisher's name was called out, and they were handed a belt buckle. Yes, a buckle for a belt.

Many American ultramarathons award their finishers such a buckle. This idiosyncrasy stems from the tradition of historic long-distance horse races. In the case of the Western States Endurance Run, that's the Tevis Cup, the predecessor of the 100-mile footrace as we know it today.

The buckle I received that afternoon in Auburn is a gorgeous, handcrafted artifact with my name engraved on its back. Olympian and Western States champion Magda Boulet handed it over to me in a classy box with a polishing cloth and a promise by Comstock Heritage, the company who created it, to repair or refinish this award for life. How beautiful is that?

My Western States 100 buckle earned a special place in my home and also in my heart. It is a real eye-catcher and sticks out from all the other medals that look so much alike that they could be from almost any race. The buckle is another unique feature that made Western States a true life event for me.

CHAPTER 52
RECOVERY AND UPCOMING ADVENTURES

My body healed faster than I expected. Within two days, I was able to walk properly again. The blisters on my soles disappeared over the following days thanks to occasional dotting treatments from Marie. Despite the intractable dirt and smell of my battered feet, she was stoked to finally get a chance to perform her well-honed blister protocol. All my other body parts seemed to function normally, which surprised me after how I'd felt during the race, especially the section up to Cal-1.

I am deeply thankful for my body and for what it allows me to do. Although the decisive part of my Western States experience was not a physical one, I wouldn't even have made it to the start line if my body hadn't functioned that well. This includes 34 weeks of demanding training, as well as surviving a tough COVID-19 infection without further damage. Thank you, body. I love you. Yes, I do.

I paused running for one full week, then picked it up again upon returning to Germany. I started with a sequence of rather uninspired 30- to 40-minute runs, but soon found myself back in moderate training. With no particular goal, though. Running gave me structure, but it didn't really spark anything inside of me.

For weeks and months after Western States, I felt both full and empty. Full of everything I had learned and experienced, but also empty because of what this race had demanded from me. I don't yet feel that I have the proper foundation to make plans or fall in love with another big running adventure. But that's ok. I'm fine with cruising along for a while and waiting until it strikes me again. I remember how long it took Lisa after her long-awaited UTMB participation in 2017 before she felt a comparable hunger for another race again. It was three years.

I also doubt that I will ever experience anything like my 2022 Western States again. I do get asked a lot if I want to go back. It's easy to answer: yes, I do want to reunite with this race one day. Not because I feel there's unfinished business. Not because I have the urge to run smarter or faster. It is an intangible feeling of belonging. An ardent wish to return to the place that has unearthed both the brightest and the darkest places inside of me. The entireness of who I am. This tour de force forever belongs to the Western State Endurance Run.

CHAPTER 53
FROM REFLECTIONS TO BOOK PAGES

n *The War of Art*, Steven Pressfield wrote: "Stevie Wonder's territory is the piano. Arnold Schwarzenegger's is the gym. When Bill Gates pulls into the parking lot at Microsoft, he's on his territory. When I sit down to write, I'm on mine."

This applies to me as well. Right next to running, writing is where I belong. It's my territory. To me, the flow state of writing is almost the same as the flow state of running.

However, just like I had never run a 100-mile race before, I'd never written a book either. It was a wonderful life project that I had been "saving for later" for years — until now. So let me briefly explain how I ended up writing the book you are holding in your hands.

The day after my Western States finish, I wanted to post a short race report on my blog to seal the deal. The next thing I knew, I had written more than 15 pages. Words just kept flowing out of me like a waterfall. It just happened. I produced an amount of content that would be absolutely inappropriate for a blog or social media post. Based on a gut feeling, I decided not to limit myself by pondering who or what these writings would be for, and just let it flow.

I ended up writing in the early morning hours, before lunch, after lunch, during lunch, at night when everyone was asleep and even on the plane back to Germany, typing these words on my tiny smartphone screen. I continued this modus operandi for weeks. It really had become an obsession, and I soon found out that reliving the past seven months and putting it on paper was very demanding and exhausting. But also cleansing. I clearly felt that this is what I had to do.

Without thinking twice, I chose the English language instead of my mother tongue. While German is quite unwieldy, I find English phonetically much more attractive, and it is way easier to get to the point. It is also an emotional safety shield. It puts a distance between the act of writing and living through every single moment. Some dialogues in particular still bring a lump in my throat when I remember them.

To give my writing a proper framework, I soon switched from a casual blogging style to full-on book authoring and started structuring my ideas in proper chapters and sections. My writing kept on progressing and page after page started piling up.

It was very unusual for me to not waste a single thought on if or how I could publish such a book until it was a complete first manuscript. But when I read through the first 200 pages I had created, I knew that I wanted to share my story with the world. Yet, the painful truth about writing is: "Nobody wants to read your sh*t." After a lesson in humility, once again from one of my favorite authors, Steven Pressfield, I completely rewrote my first manuscript to make it a truly captivating read. Not for myself, but for my readers.

Inspired by Steven Pressfield and new ideas and feedbacks, a second, a third, a fourth, and many more manuscripts followed. Basically, I started from scratch every time. I later learned that this Sisyphean nightmare is an integral part of writing a book. Professional authors call it "drafts," and they can easily add up to double digits. Thanks to the ghostwriter AJ Harper and her smart book *Write a Must-Read*, I now know that this is normal, even purposive. At one point I stopped counting drafts and simply enjoyed that *Runhundred*, a catchy title I chose along the way, was becoming better and better with every revision.

I also professionalized my personal running blog and started publishing a weekly author's newsletter to engage closely with you, my readers. Writing regular updates on my book project and occasionally conducting small surveys about your reading habits also contributed a big part to *Runhundred* becoming a reality.

I wrote this book for runners — but not exclusively for them. Even if you have never heard of the Western States Endurance Run or have until now believed that a marathon was the longest distance a human can run without dying, you might still enjoy this read. After all, this book is about a life-changing and eye-opening endeavor and the journey that led to it. Runner or not, I am sure you have made similar experiences in your life. Some of them, maybe even more intense than mine.

For a better reading flow and to bring you closer to the experience, I used some running-specific terms without further explaining them in the text. The glossary at the end of the book explains these terms.

CHAPTER 54
GRATITUDE

T his whole journey filled me with a lot of gratitude. It's one of those feelings that often briefly rushes into my mind and heart unexpectedly during any given race. As for Western States, though, this gratitude remained present for months — and maybe I'll hold onto it for years. For that reason, I want to acknowledge the following people for their roles.

It's clear to me that without Marie and Lisa, I wouldn't have made it to the finish. This is a phrase many post-race acknowledgments start with, but I am speaking literally here. After Devil's Thumb, I had made the non-negotiable decision with myself to drop out of Western States. I was absolutely convinced that this was the only way the race could end for me, and I was ready to bear all the consequences. The many ways in which my crew persuaded me to keep on running were sneaky, manipulative, insidious, and incapacitating. But they worked. And I am infinitely thankful for that.

I will always remember how I crewed for Lisa at her Tor des Géants race in 2021. It's a grueling, 205-mile (330 km) nonstop mountain race through the Aosta Valley in Italy, with roughly 82,000 feet (ca. 25,000 m) of elevation gain and loss that needs to be finished in less than 150 hours. Lisa was mentally and physically devastated many times. However, the only method I could come up with to convince her to continue the race despite all the pain and fatigue was straight up lying to her face. I lied to her about how far it was to the next aid station, and I lied to her that she was moving fast enough that she wouldn't have to run through another night. And yes, it worked. We'd agreed before the race that small lies are okay if they serve the greater purpose. But my crude and dull interventions were a total disgrace compared to the sophisticated and loving way Marie and Lisa influenced me to continue running. Short and sweet: it was a masterpiece of crewing.

My deepest gratitude also goes out to the remainder of my Western States crew: Michi, Henning, and Christiane. Although they couldn't execute the job they had been originally assigned to, I still benefited from their support tremendously. In the weeks of preparation, and even more during my COVID-ridden race week, their contribution to my overall experience was huge. They truly had my back by cooking, cracking jokes, shopping for groceries, researching and sharing their knowledge about the race, and most importantly, by staying positive even when times were tough. Michi, Henning, and Christiane were out there on the trail with me in spirit all the time, even though they were not there physically.

There's one more name that pops up rather frequently in this book: Karim Ramadan. Without his smartly tailored preparation and constant support, I would not be a Western States finisher. The seven months of training were a wild ride, and there were times when I doubted my abilities as a runner and questioned the process instead of trusting it. Karim stayed calm and focused when I did not and guided me through the many highs and lows. He also equipped me with a set of mental skills that go far beyond the realm of running. He's not only made me a better runner, but also a better human. I am very much looking forward to tackling the next running projects with him.

"Don't worry. You will come back at night!" That's just one of many uplifting things fellow Western States runners said to me during the race. They encouraged me not only when I was going through hell, but also when I was feeling great. Brief chats and words of motivation were omnipresent. The cama-raderie and positive energy among the participants were exceptional. Maybe it's because there are only a handful of runners every year. It could also be because this race means so much to everyone, albeit for different reasons. Either way, I am deeply thankful for the great spirit among everyone who ran Western States in 2022.

And finally, there is the Western States Endurance Run itself. For many reasons, it's a race like no other in the world. However, there is one particular quality that makes it abso-lutely exceptional and stand out from the rest. And that is the warm-hearted family spirit and total commitment of all the volunteers and officials who keep the wheels on the wagon. Entering each of the 20 aid stations felt like coming home. Within seconds, you were looking into smiling faces and a friendly person asked how you were doing and what you needed. In addition to that, I can only speculate how many

DNFs are being prevented by aid station captains and volunteers every year. Surely, a lot. I still get a feeling of enlightenment when I recall the old lady's words at Cal-1: "You get out of this chair. Now. This is Western States!"

Thank you. I owe you much more than just a Western States finish.

100

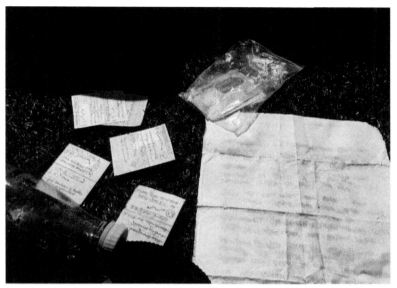

My **race notes** and **love letters** from Lisa that I carried with me all the way from Olympic Valley to Auburn. *(Henning Lenertz)*

Moment of care and love with Lisa at the finish. *(Henning Lenertz)*

Blisters on my feet. Luzia Buehler (left) said, I shouldn't worry about it, it will be fine again soon, and she was right. *(Henning Lenertz)*

Proud Western States finisher with his **belt buckle**. *(Lisa Mehl)*

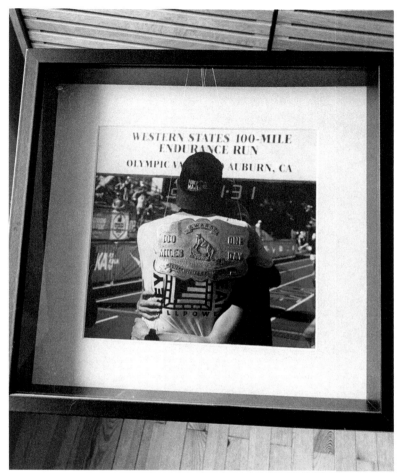

I found a special place for my Western States **belt buckle**. I framed it and put it on our kitchen wall. *(Chris Zehetleitner)*

I spent the last few days in California relaxing and recharging my batteries. We hiked a tiny portion of the Pacific Crest Trail (PCT) on that day and ended up at **Winnemucca Lake**, south of Lake Tahoe. *(Lisa Mehl)*

FINAL THOUGHTS

> "The way, the truth, the light. I walk through the
> darkness to remember the light."
>
> — TIMOTHY OLSON

RUNNING WITH YOUR HEART

Running an ultramarathon is always an intense experience. Finishing it is a great accomplishment. As I said at the beginning of this book, I am not the one to tell you how to do, either. And despite their achievement, every ultrarunner eventually experiences an empty body and a mind shattered by disruptive thoughts. It's woven into the DNA of this sport. And it's precisely the point where something else, something non-physical, is needed to keep on moving forward. A grand force from deep inside, a quasi-magic source of energy that does not show up in our everyday lives. It lifts your spirits, encourages you to find hope in hopelessness, and grants you the chance to run after you're long done with running. It's your truth and your purpose.

This power has many names. I call it **running with your heart,** and it makes the impossible possible.

I had the great luck to discover this power at my Western States race, and it changed my life forever. While I know that it will probably be months, if not years, until I draw from that power again, it is still highly inspiring to know it exists. To me, it appears to be that "something bigger than us" thing that religious people sometimes use to picture their god.

Running with your heart reveals what's left when there's nothing left. But it also means to dream freely and aim high regarding your running goals. Sure, a solid preparation helps a lot and there are many challenges before and during a race that are best to be tackled with a clear focus and a sharp mind. But listening to your heart and following the path where it leads you is the foundation your greatest personal running accomplishments are built upon. If it wasn't for your heart, why would you run at all? In other words, it's good to have a plan. Yet when the heat is on the street, or the trail, for that matter, you're not going anywhere without your heart.

Running with your heart can also stand for liberating yourself from any external and internal limitations. Sometimes it seems like we are more often told what we cannot do instead of being encouraged to do the things we love. If we're only playing it safe all the time, we cannot thrive, and we cannot evolve. It's a brave act to break down those barriers of doubt. But it's almost always worth it. If not for a great experience, then at least for an important life lesson.

Finally, running with your heart means running and living in the present moment. Or as Addie Bracy puts it in her book *Mental Training for Ultrarunning*:

"Run the mile you're in."

After all, for me, running is about finding meaning in seemingly meaningless actions. How would one single step bring me any closer to the finish line? How would one mile entirely change the outcome of a 100-mile race? How would a foot race change my life forever? The answer lies within. There is great meaning in everything we do. Therefore also in running. Sometimes it just takes some time to find out what that meaning is. It all starts with running for running's sake.

EPILOGUE

WESTERN STATES REMINDED ME THAT WE ARE ALL HUMANS

We are imperfect and fragile beings, who
stumble rather than march through life.

With every step, we carry all the pain we ever
experienced in life. But also all the love
and joy.

We study tenaciously to find out we know
nothing.

We never truly believe in ourselves until everything falls apart, and we have to start from
scratch.

We love and support others selflessly and get even more love in return.

We fear facing or revealing our weaknesses and dark sides for no good reason.

We strive for perfection but fail terribly.

We lose hope and look for salvation in giving up on ourselves.

Our bodies bend for a long time, but eventually break. Then they heal again when we least expect it.

We are often late to the realization that life and running are not about numbers and calculations, but about the beating of our hearts and what that rhythm means. Or, in the case of Western States champion Ruth Croft, about dinosaurs.

YES, WE ARE HUMANS. AND THAT'S A WONDERFUL THING.

This race has taken everything from me. And then it gave me back more than I have ever possessed. Western States changed my life, and I am deeply thankful for that.

100

ABOUT THE AUTHOR

Chris Zehetleitner is a 44-year-old writer, ultrarunner, cat lover, coffee connoisseur and former touring musician and music professional from Munich, Germany. He is the founder and owner of the running clothing brand *Willpower* and a couple of other more or less visible side hustles. Chris runs the *Das Z*

(Photo by Chris Drüke)

Letter running blog and newsletter and occasionally contributes stories to *Like the Wind Magazine*, *Runner's World*, *Laufzeit* and other running media. He started running rather late in his life, when he was 34, and he hasn't stopped since. Together with his wife Lisa, he enjoys life and running to the fullest and looks forward to many more exciting running projects in the future.

Sign up for the author's mailing list at **dasz.substack.com**

facebook.com/czehetleitner

instagram.com/chrisxwillpower

amazon.com/author/chris-zehetleitner

ABOUT THE WESTERN STATES ENDURANCE RUN

The Western States Endurance Run (also known as the "Western States 100") is a 100.2-mile (161 km) ultra-marathon, the oldest and most iconic in the world. It takes place each June in the Sierra Nevada Mountains in California. The racecourse starts at high altitude in Olympic Valley and gradually descents into Auburn, a small town in Placer County, midway between Reno, Nevada, and Sacramento, California.

Participants of the race have to climb 18,090 feet (5,500 m) and descend 22,970 feet (7,000 m). It looks doable on paper, but it's grueling in reality. Besides running at high altitude through rugged backcountry terrain, runners also have to deal with the intense heat, one of the major challenges of the Western States Endurance Run. The temperature can reach up to 104 °F (40 °C), and long stretches of the racecourse are fully exposed to the sun.

The race has a strict 30-hour cutoff time to be recognized as an official finisher and receive a bronze belt buckle. Runners who finish the race in under 24 hours receive a silver belt buckle.

While the original Western States Trail was created and used by the Indigenous Washoe and Nisenan peoples for thousands of years, it was in the nineteenth century wrested from them by white explorers and settlers who exploited the land for gold and silver and displaced or wiped out the Indigenous tribes. In 1955, Wendell T. Robie turned the trail into a horse race called the Tevis Cup, proving that horses could cover the 100 miles between Tahoe City and Auburn in one day. Seventeen years later, 20 U.S. soldiers attempted to hike the trail one day ahead of the Tevis Cup. Seven of them made it, with times ranging from 44:54 to 46:49 hours. Two years after that, in 1974, Tevis Cup veteran and current Western States 100 legend Gordy Ainsleigh repeated this attempt but managed to finish his run in 23:42 hours. With that, the Western States Endurance Run was born. Its first official edition was in 1977 with a starter field of 14 men, increasing to 63 starters in 1978, including the first woman, Pat Smythe, to finish Western States. Just one year later, 143 men from 21 states and three foreign countries participated in the race. In the following years, the interest and application numbers consistently increased.

Since 1984, only 369 participants are allowed to run Western States 100 each year. More than 6,000 runners first qualify by running a given qualifying race, usually a 100-km or 100-mile distance. Then they apply for the notorious lottery that selects only 267 people to run the race. An additional 102 runners are automatic entrants because they finished top 10 in the previous year, scored a first or second place at one of the main sponsor's so-called Golden Ticket Races, are members of the Board of Directors, have finished Western States nine times going for tenth (or 18- and 19- time finishers going for 19 and 20), or have been selected as Special Consideration or Silver Legend because of their outstanding work and support for the race. There are also ten transferable entries offered through an on-site charity raffle for the WSER Foundation. The race organizers furthermore established a wait list which gives hope to an additional 75 lottery winning applicants to move up.

The course record for men stands at 14:09:28 hours and was set by Jim Walmsley in 2019 and the women's record is 15:29:33 hours, set by Courtney Dauwalter in 2023. Alongside the UTMB in Chamonix, France, the Western States Endurance Run is the most competitive and most sought-after ultrarunning event in the world. Almost without exception, Western States sees the most outstanding athletic performances in our sport every year. It repeatedly redefines what is possible in ultra trail running and endurance sports in general. To almost every ultrarunner, it is the biggest dream and greatest honor to be a part of it.

100

ACKNOWLEDGMENTS

Without the following people, this book would not be a book, but a series of trivial blog articles and Instagram posts. I owe you all a lot.

Firstly, the biggest thank you to Lisa for sharing every single Western States moment with me, before, during and afterward. Also for having my back while writing this book.

Moreover, thanks to our cats, Harry and Toto, for joining me on early morning or late-night writing sessions and reminding me when it was time to eat. For all of us, of course.

To my Western States crew, Christiane, Michi, Henning, Lisa, and Marie for sharing the same passion. Not just for Western States, but for running in general. I am deeply thankful for discussing, reflecting, and thus solidifying the full experience with all of you. We've been chatting about Western States for days and weeks, even after the race was long over. Without this precious exchange, a lot of the stories in this book would have been lost.

To Henning in particular for the great foreword. I will do the same for you once you write your own book about Western States.

To Emi for her detailed feedback on the book in its early stages and identifying phrases only her grandma would use. I am truly not a native speaker, and your input made these words much less quirky.

To Christine for bringing this book to an entirely new level. Your profound editing experience helped me avoid a good number of rookie mistakes and added great value to the story. I truly enjoyed working with you.

To Alessandro for the great cover artwork and graphics. If it is true that a picture is worth a thousand words, then yours are worth a million.

To the Willpower Athletes for being a continuous source of inspiration and the best friends in the world.

To Björn and Christian, who encouraged me to start running in 2013. I know that neither of you did it deliberately, but you said just the right thing at just the right time.

To Karim for all the quotes of wisdom that found their way into this book without explicit permission. I hope you don't mind.

To Scott Jurek for being a great inspiration as a runner and author, and for the motivational boost at Quarry Road.

To all the wonderful volunteers, race officials, medics, rangers, and fellow runners who gave me something to write about in the first place.

And finally, to all of you, the readers of this book. After all, I can't expect everyone to care about my Western States experience. I'm honored that you read my book.

Thank you all. Sincerely.

GLOSSARY

Although I doubt that many non-runners will pick up this book, I still want to explain a few technical terms that I used in my writing. These definitions are my own words and may differ from Wikipedia or whatever additional source of information you use to look them up.

Bib number: Mandatory identification number at race events, usually printed on a small sheet of Tyvek and affixed to the runners' tops. Often also equipped with a time tracking sensor

Cal-1, Cal-2 & Cal-3: The old and established names of the 12th, 13th, and 14th aid stations on Cal Street, also called the Cal Loop, of the Western States Endurance Run. Their new names are Dardanelles, Peachstone, and Ford's Bar, respectively

CCC (*"Courmayeur - Champex-Lac - Chamonix"*): 100 kilometer distance as part of the UTMB event

Cutoff: A time limit instituted by the organizers of a race. If a runner doesn't finish the race or pass by a certain point, such as an aid station, they will not be recognized as an official finisher. At Western States, the cutoff is 30 hours

DNF (*"Did Not Finish"*): The act of prematurely ending a race before crossing the finish line

D+ / D- : The cumulative elevation gain and loss during trail or mountain running

GI stress: Gastrointestinal stress, issues with the digestive system such as nausea, vomiting, or diarrhea

PB (*"Personal Best"*) / **PR** (*"Personal Record"*): A runner's best time result on any given distance

Skyrace: A running event in steep mountainous terrain, usually exceeding 6,600 feet (2000 m) with an incline of up to 30%

Starter bag: A goodie bag filled with gifts and promotional items handed out to race participants before the start

Tevis Cup: A traditional long-distance horse race founded in 1955, proving that horses could cover the 100 miles between Tahoe City and Auburn in one day. It is the predecessor and origin of the Western States Endurance Run as we know it today

Tapering: The gradual and structured reduction of training load before a race

Ultramarathon: Any running distance longer than 42.195 km (26.22 miles), the traditional length of a road marathon. It could be a 50k, 50-mile, 100k, or 100-mile race — or even longer

UTMB (*"Ultra-Trail du Mont-Blanc"*): Biggest ultrarunning event in the world and the name of its 100-mile race

Vertical K: Vertical kilometer, a particular type of skyrace in which runners run uphill and finish on top of a mountain while gaining 1000 m of elevation in less than 5 kilometers

Willpower Athletes: A small group of like-minded runners and friends gathered around the running clothing brand Willpower

100

SOURCES

Bracy, Addie. *Mental Training for Ultrarunning: Your Psychological Skills Guidebook for Ultra Success*. Human Kinetics, 2021.

Harper, A.J. *Write a Must-Read: Craft a Book That Changes Lives: Including Your Own*. Page Two Books, Inc, 2022.

Jurek, Scott. *Eat and Run: My Unlikely Journey to Ultramarathon Greatness*. Houghton Mifflin Harcourt, 2012.

Koop, Jason. *Training Essentials for Ultrarunning – Second Edition*. Koop Endurance Services, LLC, 2021.

Murakami, Haruki. *What I Talk About When I Talk About Running*. Vintage Books International, 2009.

Pressfield, Steven. *Nobody Wants to Read Your Sh*t: And Other Tough-Love Truths to Make You a Better Writer*. Black Irish Entertainment, 2018.

Pressfield, Steven. *The War of Art: Break Through the Blocks and Win Your Inner Creative Battles*. Black Irish Entertainment, 2002.

Western States Endurance Run. *Official Website*. www.wser.org. Accessed September 2022 to August 2023.

100

Thanks for joining me on my Western States journey. Enjoyed reading Runhundred? If you have a moment to spare, I would really appreciate a short review. Your help in spreading the word is gratefully received.

Printed in Great Britain
by Amazon

37456961R00149